PHILIP NATION

LifeWay Press®
Nashville, Tennessee

ISBN 978-1-4158-5287-3
Item 005035528

Dewey decimal classification: 220.07
Subject headings: BIBLE—STUDY \ GOD

This book is the resource for course CG-1453 in the subject area
Personal Life in the Christian Growth Study Plan.

Cover illustration: Mac Premo

Scripture quotations are taken from the Holman Christian Standard Bible®,
copyright © 1999, 2000, 2002, 2003 by Holman Bible Publishers.

To order additional copies of this resource, write to LifeWay Church Resources
Customer Service; One LifeWay Plaza; Nashville, TN 37234-0113;
fax 615.251.5933; phone toll free 800.458.2772; e-mail *orderentry@lifeway.com;*
order online at *www.lifeway.com;* or visit the LifeWay Christian Store serving you.

Printed in the United States of America

Adult Ministry Publishing
LifeWay Church Resources
One LifeWay Plaza
Nashville, TN 37234-0152

Contents

Introducing Philip Nation 4

Preface 5

Introducing *Live in the Word* 7

Week 1: Treasuring the Word 10
Day 1: Loving God's Word 12
Day 2: Inspired by God 14
Day 3: Eternally True 16
Day 4: Trustworthy in Every Way 18
Day 5: Loving the Author 20
Session 1 22

Week 2: The Authority of God's Word 24
Day 1: God's Power Displayed 26
Day 2: The Call to Salvation 28
Day 3: Uncovering What Is Hidden. 30
Day 4: Our Weapon in Battle. 32
Day 5: God's Word: Our Authority 34
Session 2 36

Week 3: Transformed by the Word 38
Day 1: Teaching 40
Day 2: Rebuking. 42
Day 3: Correcting 44
Day 4: Training. 46
Day 5: Equipped for Every Good Work. . . 48
Session 3 50

Week 4: How to Study the Word. 52
Day 1: Asking the Right Questions 54
Day 2: Reading for All Its Worth. 56
Day 3: Meditating and Memorizing. 58
Day 4: Understanding Genres 60
Day 5: Two Major Themes 62
Session 4 64

Week 5: Living the Word. 66
Day 1: Listening, Then Doing 68
Day 2: Love That Shows 70
Day 3: Deep Devotion 72
Day 4: Praying the Word 74
Day 5: Solid Decision Making 76
Session 5 78

Week 6: Spreading the Word. 80
Day 1: Leading the Next Generation 82
Day 2: Generous Conversations 84
Day 3: Calling the Wayward Home 86
Day 4: Caring for Outsiders 88
Day 5: Raising Up Leaders 90
Session 6 92

Discipleship Helps 94

Leader Guide 108
The Growing Disciples Series 110
Scripture-Memory Cards. 113

Introducing Philip Nation

Philip Nation began following Christ at 7 years of age. After many conversations with his parents, he knelt beside the family sofa one Sunday morning to receive Christ as his Savior. Philip responded to God's call to full-time ministry at the age of 16 and preached his first sermon soon after. During his college and seminary days, he served in several part-time positions leading youth ministries in his hometown of Birmingham, Alabama. He earned a bachelor of arts from Samford University and a master of divinity from Beeson Divinity School. During his formative years of ministry, Philip was blessed to be personally discipled by a great friend who taught him how to study God's Word and pass along its truth to others.

Philip has participated in a variety of ministries. He served as the pastor of churches in rural and suburban settings in three states. He also served as the minister of education at First Baptist Church in Jonesboro, Georgia. In 2005 Philip led an effort to plant a new missional church in north metro Atlanta. Currently, he serves as Director of Ministry Development at LifeWay Christian Resources.

Philip is the coauthor of *Compelled by Love: The Most Excellent Way to Missional Living* with Ed Stetzer (New Hope Publishers, 2008). He is also the author of the LifeWay small-group study *Compelled by Love: The Journey to Missional Living*. Additionally, he has contributed to numerous articles and other books written by friends.

Philip and his wonderful wife, Angie, make their home near Nashville, Tennessee, with their two incredible sons, Andrew and Chris.

Preface

The Bible is unlike any other book that man could ever read, write, or dream of. Its beautiful nature causes the soul to soar and the conscience to sear. Its mysterious nature boggles the mind, and its plain truth confronts the heart. The Bible is an overly gracious gift from God to humanity.

The Scriptures contain 66 books written by more than three dozen authors. It was written in three different languages and in numerous styles for its diverse audiences. The Bible's lines were penned on three continents over a period of 1,500 years. And still it has only one main character, only one great purpose, and only one epic story.

Seeking to be a diligent student of God's Word, I have often failed. But with God's message of personal grace and kindness, He always welcomes me back to His Word to hear from His heart once again. Perhaps you find yourself in a position of—
  • learning to study God's Word for the first time;
  • wanting to increase your understanding of God's Word and your ability to learn from it;
  • returning to God and seeking His guidance for living out your relationship with Him.

In my spiritual journey I have been in all three of those positions, and I have found that God's voice is present every time I come to His Word. No matter what our motivation is for reading the Bible, God speaks to us through His Word and promises that the Scriptures will accomplish whatever He desires for our lives.

Growing up in the 19th century, George Müller lived immorally in his youth but was pressed into religious studies by his father to earn a decent salary through the state church. Through his study of God's Word, he came to personal faith in Christ and was spiritually transformed by the power of the gospel.

Müller eventually moved to London to do missionary work. He and his wife began founding orphanages in the 1830s. Throughout his lifetime Müller existed solely on prayer and unsolicited donations. Each time there was a need, he studied God's

Word and prayed. And in every circumstance God provided whatever was needed. What could have possibly so transformed an otherwise selfish man to embark on such an epic journey of care for others?

Müller explained how his spiritual transformation occurred in this way:

> The vigor of our Spiritual Life will be in exact proportion to the place held by the Bible in our life and thoughts. I solemnly state this from the experience of fifty-four years. ... The first three years after conversion I neglected the Word of God. Since I began to search it dilligently the blessing has been wonderful. ... I have read the Bible through one hundred times, and always with increasing delight. Each time it seems like a new book to me. ... Great has been the blessing from consecutive, diligent, daily study. I look upon it as a lost day when I have not had a good time over the Word of God.[1]

Müller's explanation for the effectiveness of his life's work always pointed toward the wisdom of God. His life was publicly defined by his compassion for the most powerless of society—orphans. His private life was defined by his dependency on God, as if he were an orphan himself who was cared for by the Heavenly Father.

Müller said of a Christian who does not value God's Word: "That believer makes a fatal mistake who for any cause neglects the prayerful study of the word of God. To read God's holy book, by it search one's self, and turn it into prayer and so into holy living, is the one great secret of growth in grace and godliness."[2]

Knowing the preciousness of the Scriptures, Müller was determined to put into practice what he learned of God's character and the church's mission. To that end he devoted 64 years of his life to act according to God's Word. During that time he began seven day schools that helped a total of 81,501 children. He distributed 1,989,266 Bibles and aided 115 foreign missionaries. All in all, he took in 10,024 orphans and spent 988,829 pounds sterling on homes for them. It is said of Müller that "he believed what he found in the word of God, and by His grace sought to act accordingly, and thus again records that he was blessed abundantly and his peace and joy in the Holy Ghost increased more and more."[3]

Lives like Müller's are possible for all believers because we have access to the same God. We can witness His great kingdom arrive in power as we study and live according to His Word.

Introducing Live in the Word

Growing Disciples: Live in the Word is part of the Growing Disciples Series (see p. 110). This series of self-paced, interactive Bible studies introduces you to six disciplines illustrated by the Disciple's Cross that was first developed and popularized by Avery Willis in *MasterLife: A Biblical Process for Growing Disciples*. Take a look at the diagram of the Disciple's Cross below to see where the discipline of Live in the Word fits in the spiritual life of a follower of Jesus Christ.

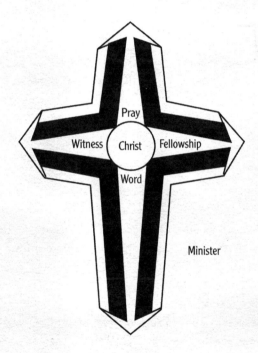

Live in the Word is one of the disciplines in the vertical crossbar designating your relationship with God. As we begin a study of this discipline, let's first take a brief look at all six.

THE SIX DISCIPLINES OF THE DISCIPLE'S CROSS

1. Abide in Christ

To abide in Christ is central to all of the disciplines. Jesus invites you to a love relationship with Himself. He wants you to know, understand, and live according to His commands so that you can experience the best life God has to offer you. His Word and prayer are the tools through which we speak to Him and

He speaks to us. By abiding in Christ, you receive all the life and vitality you need to be filled with joy and fruitfulness.

2. Live in the Word

God has revealed Himself, His purposes, and His ways in the Bible. He has given guidelines for an abundant and meaningful life. Jesus set an example for us by knowing Scripture and applying it in His daily living. You will learn to read, study, memorize, and meditate on God's Word in order to know Him and understand His commands, His purposes, and His ways. Then you can live your life in a way that pleases Him and is abundantly full.

3. Pray in Faith

Prayer is not just a religious activity; it describes a relationship with a person. Prayer is your intimate communion with God. In prayer you experience a loving relationship, you receive God's counsel and directions, you respond in praise and worship, you receive cleansing through confession, and you work together with God through petition for yourself and intercession for others.

4. Fellowship with Believers

When Jesus saved you, He placed you in the body of Christ with other believers. In relationships with other believers, you receive help to be all God wants you to be; and God uses you to meet the needs of the rest of the body. Together we grow strong in our faith, and we accomplish the kingdom work of Christ in the world for which He died.

5. Witness to the World

Jesus came with an assignment to seek and to save those who are lost. He went to the cross to reconcile a lost world to God the Father. He has given to us the ministry and message of reconciliation so that others can experience a saving relationship with God. We have both the privilege and the responsibility to witness about Christ to a lost and dying world around us.

6. Minister to Others

Jesus modeled a life of service for His disciples and for us. He did not come to be served but to serve others. His call for us is to a life of service to those who are needy, both in the body of Christ and in the world that has yet to believe. When we love and serve others who are needy, we show our love for Christ Himself; and God uses that service to build up the body of Christ.

The Growing Disciples Series provides a six-week study for each of the six disciplines in the Disciple's Cross. *The Call to Follow Christ,* the first book in the series, introduces the six disciplines for new and growing believers. Though you would benefit from studying that course first, it is not a prerequisite. A person can study the individual disciplines in any order, based on interest and spiritual need. The goal of discipleship is to grow strong and balanced in each of these six disciplines. Because new believers need to understand the importance of handling and obeying the Word of God, this can be a valuable study whether it comes first or later.

SMALL-GROUP STUDY OF *LIVE IN THE WORD*

Although you could study this book alone, finding a group of friends to join you in a journey through the study will most likely bear more fruit in your life. Interacting with the Bible is a personal journey but not a private one.

If you are the person who will lead the small-group sessions, I have included a brief leader guide for you, beginning on page 108. A guide for each small-group session is included at the end of each week's devotionals.

PERSONAL STUDY OF *LIVE IN THE WORD*

This book is designed as an interactive study. Each week will guide you through five daily devotionals and will offer an opportunity for you to memorize a short verse. The interactive questions are written for your benefit, so take full advantage of them. The devotionals will prepare you for the small-group study each week. Each day's devotional can last as long as you wish to explore the lesson. I hope you will find yourself enthralled by God's Word as He speaks to you through it, so that you want to spend more and more time in Bible study.

Although I have been blessed to be the author of this study, it is the product of countless other believers who have taught and shown me how to live in the Word. I would like to thank some of them: my wife, Angie; my sons, Andrew and Chris; Mom and Dad; Bill Overstreet; Doug Sager; Larry and Anna Lawrence; Lanny and Isabel Loe; Rush Harrison; Charles Q. Carter; Timothy George; Jeff Langley; Tim Wolfe; Ed Stetzer; Henry Blackaby; and especially Matthew Roskam. I pray that you will also find yourself surrounded by such a great cloud of witnesses to the power of God's Word as you faithfully embrace and follow its teachings.

1. Henry H. Halley, *Halley's Bible Handbook: An Abbreviated Bible Commentary* (Grand Rapids, MI: Zondervan, 1965), 4.
2. A.T. Pierson, *George Müller of Bristol and His Witness to a Prayer-Hearing God* (Old Tappan, NJ: Fleming H. Revell, 1899), 96.
3. Ibid, 300.

Week 1

Treasuring
the Word

"How I love Your teaching!
It is my meditation
all day long."
Psalm 119:97

Treasuring the Word

Bibliophile: a person who collects or has a great love of books.

I admit it—I am one. My home office is lined with books that are old, new, serious, fun, theological, historical, biographical, and fictional. I love great books and sometimes not-so-great ones. But none can dare compete with the beauty of God's Word.

Through this study I hope you will learn to treasure God's Word. This gift from our Heavenly Father serves as—
• a personal message about God's character and kingdom;
• a public declaration of God's goodness and desire to redeem fallen humanity and creation;
• a transformative instrument that reveals how God changes our lives and how people are to relate to one another.

God's Word is no ordinary book on a shelf or decoration for a coffee table. It is eternal, inspired, and worth every moment of time we dedicate to it.

OVERVIEW OF WEEK 1
Day 1: Loving God's Word
Day 2: Inspired by God
Day 3: Eternally True
Day 4: Trustworthy in Every Way
Day 5: Loving the Author

VERSE TO MEMORIZE
"How I love Your teaching! It is my meditation all day long" (Psalm 119:97).

DISCIPLESHIP HELP FOR WEEK 1
"Outline of the Bible" (p. 94)

Day 1 • Loving God's Word

. . . .

God's Word for Today
"How I love Your teaching! It is my meditation all day long."
Psalm 119:97

Read and meditate on "God's Word for Today" (this week's verse to memorize) in the margin. Spend a moment in prayer as you begin today's lesson. Remove the Scripture-memory card for week 1 from the back of your book and begin committing this verse to memory.

Humans are wired to love. We naturally want to find someone or something for which we feel affection. Sometimes we focus on eternal things and sometimes on the temporary. But we always look for an object for our affection.

The primary focus of our love should be God. He is the Author of life and the only One who saves us from our sin. We should also love Him because He has chosen to speak to us. It is an awe-inspiring thought: the everlasting God has spoken truth to those He created in a temporary place so that they can receive eternal life. For that reason we should love God and all of His gifts to us, especially His Word.

We love the Bible because God uses it to reveal Himself to us. God has chosen to use the Scriptures as our primary source of understanding about His character and His will. Through God's perfect words we gain insight into everyday living and eternal life. Because of what Scripture does in our lives and the One who has given it to us, we should deeply love this great gift from our Heavenly Father. ~~What God IS.~~

Psalm 7:17
"I will thank the LORD for His righteousness."

Psalm 100:5
"The LORD is good, and His love is eternal; His faithfulness endures through all generations."

Colossians 1:11
"May you be strengthened with all power, according to His glorious might."

1 John 4:8
"God is love."

1. Read the following verses and record the aspects of God's character that are named.
   Psalm 7:17: _righteousnes_   Psalm 100:5: _good Eternal Love_
   Colossians 1:11: _glorious might_   1 John 4:8: _Love_

We love the Bible because God uses it to change us. As we study and obey God's Word every day, it changes us. The Bible is a trustworthy guide for every decision we make about the greatest challenges, the most intense temptations, and the smallest details of life. In some measure the Word of God addresses every circumstance we face in life. The Father has graciously and clearly spoken so that we can find direction for our lives.

② **Read Psalm 119:97-104. Place a check mark beside the effects God's Word has on us when we truly love it and spend time with it.**
○ A lack of direction ☑ Wisdom ☑ Understanding
☑ The right path ○ Gullibility ☑ A love for truth

Our love for God's Word should always increase as it makes a consistently larger impact on our lives. As we read, study, and obey, we are changed. The more we are changed, the more we love the Word. The more we love the Word, the more time we spend in the Word. The more time we spend in the Word, the more we are changed.

③ **Read the following verses in Psalm 119 and circle each word describing an action or a reaction we are to have to the Scriptures.**
"Never take the word of truth from my mouth, for I (hope) in Your judgments. I will always (keep) Your law, forever and ever. I will (walk) freely in an open place because I seek Your precepts. I will (speak) of Your decrees before kings and not be ashamed. I (delight) in Your commands, which I love. I will (lift up) my hands to Your commands, (which I love, and will meditate) on Your statutes" (Psalm 119:43-48).

④ **Read Psalm 19:7-11. List some characteristics of God's Word.**

Perfect, trustworthy, right, radiant, Pure, Sure, More Precious than gold, sweeter than honey. Refreshing, enduring, Firm

In *The Call to Follow Christ* Claude King reflected on Psalm 19:7-11 by stating, "God's words are trustworthy, perfect, right, radiant, pure, enduring, reliable, righteous, desirable, and sweeter than honey! They can revive you, make you wise and glad, and enlighten you. They can warn you for your own protection. When you obey them, 'there is great reward.' … I want to help you live *in* God's Word AND live *by* God's Word."[1]

As citizens of God's kingdom, we are blessed to have a King who has spoken to us. As members of God's family, we are children who have heard from our Heavenly Father. As ambassadors for Christ, we are encouraged to know that the One who offers redemption has sent us out with His words of life.

Spend time in prayer thanking God for His Word. Ask Him to increase your appreciation and understanding through this study.

Psalm 119:97-104
"How I love Your teaching! It is my meditation all day long. Your command makes me wiser than my enemies, for it is always with me. I have more insight than all my teachers because Your decrees are my meditation. I understand more than the elders because I obey Your precepts. I have kept my feet from every evil path to follow Your word. I have not turned from Your judgments, for You Yourself have instructed me. How sweet Your word is to my taste—sweeter than honey to my mouth. I gain understanding from Your precepts; therefore I hate every false way."

1. Claude King, *The Call to Follow Christ* (Nashville: LifeWay Press, 2006), 34.

Day 2 • Inspired by God

Read and meditate on "God's Word for Today" in the margin. Spend a moment in prayer as you begin today's lesson.

God's Word for Today

"All Scripture is inspired by God and is profitable for teaching, for rebuking, for correcting, for training in righteousness."
2 Timothy 3:16

In our world God has provided **general revelation*** of Himself. When we look at the order of creation, the heavens above, and the earth beneath our feet, the imprint of God's hand is apparent. Even the conscience, which is common to all people, speaks of a created order and therefore a Creator.

God has also given us **special revelation***—the Scriptures. The Bible is the written revelation of God's character and activity. It is not an ordinary book. Though penned by human hands, it is different from all other books because its source is God instead of human beings. People can offer lofty ideas and soaring goals for life. But only God can reveal Himself and objective truth. We are limited in our knowledge and can only comment subjectively on our circumstances by offering our opinions. In contrast, our eternal God speaks as the fountainhead of all truth.

General revelation: God's making known His nature and purpose through nature and history

Special revelation: God's making known His nature and purpose through the written Word

Genre: a type or category of writing having a particular form, content, or technique. Examples are history, poetry, prophecy, and letters.

(1) **Read Proverbs 4:7-9 in the margin. Why should we strive to gain the wisdom of the Scriptures?**

Give you understanding, exalt you, beauty, honor mercy

Many people wonder how we received the Bible. It was written in numerous places by numerous authors and in numerous **genres***; yet it tells one story—the story of God's love and redemption through His Son, Jesus. Only by divine inspiration could this be accomplished.

Proverbs 4:7-9

"Wisdom is supreme—so get wisdom. And whatever else you get, get understanding. Cherish her, and she will exalt you; if you embrace her, she will honor you. She will place a garland of grace on your head; she will give you a crown of beauty."

"God's Word for Today," 2 Timothy 3:16, states that "all Scripture is inspired by God." The literal translation of that phrase in the Greek language is "breathed out by God." The Scriptures naturally come from God the same way breath comes from us. Though physically written down by human hands, the words of Scripture were perfectly inspired by God.

For example, when Matthew wrote the Gospel of Matthew, he did so under God's inspiration. God used Matthew's personality and perspective to communicate the life of Jesus Christ. But at all times God's message was perfectly preserved, even though it was told through an imperfect human. God used Matthew's perspective as a Jewish man to write a Gospel that would clearly communicate the life of Christ to Jewish people.

Solomon's writing of Ecclesiastes is an example from the Old Testament. Throughout the book God authoritatively speaks through Solomon's cynical view of life, wealth, pleasure, and accomplishment. In the midst of Solomon's search for meaning, God teaches us that life's meaning is found only in relation to His kingdom purposes.

(2) Read Romans 15:4 in the margin. What is the ultimate purpose for which God has given us the Scriptures? ~~for our instructions~~
Have Hope!

(3) Describe a current crisis your are facing (for example, job, finances, marriage, or temptation). How will knowing that the Bible is divinely inspired give you hope as you apply the Word to your crisis?
Havin trouble with my rodemean sister. It will help you by giving you ideas on what to do

Romans 15:4
"Whatever was written before was written for our instruction, so that through our endurance and through the encouragement of the Scriptures we may have hope."

Human history is littered with books that claim to be filled with spiritual truth. Each major religious system has a text that its followers use as a guide. Only the Bible has endured the test of time and the test of prophecy. When God promised that a nation would fall, a plague would come, or the Messiah would arrive, He was always correct. Because God divinely inspired and preserved Scripture to our day, we can trust all it says. As a whole, the Bible is the truth, not merely a book that contains some truth.

General revelation gives us an idea of God's existence and His impact on our existence. The specific revelation found in the Bible, however, is God's message to us that reveals exactly who He is and what He is doing. It is the full revelation that God desires for us to have.

(4) How is the Bible different from books of religion and philosophy?
The bible is an instructional guide for humans to follow

(5) How have you found the Bible to be a trustworthy guide for your life?
By it telling me how to handle tough situations the right way

As a whole, the Bible is the truth, not merely a book that contains some truth.

Day 3 • Eternally True

God's Word for Today

"By obedience to the truth, having purified yourselves for sincere love of the brothers, love one another earnestly from a pure heart, since you have been born again—not of perishable seed but of imperishable—through the living and enduring word of God. For All flesh is like grass, and all its glory like a flower of the grass. The grass withers, and the flower drops off, but the word of the Lord endures forever. And this is the word that was preached as the gospel to you."
1 Peter 1:22-25

Read and meditate on "God's Word for Today" in the margin. Spend a moment in prayer as you begin today's lesson.

We live in a hurry-up-and-get-it-done world. Deadlines loom around us. Work calendars scream for our attention. There is always someplace to go and something to do. We exist in a never-ending world of work that can be summed up with one word—*temporary*.

God's Word is different. It is eternal in its scope. In fact, 1 Peter 1:22-25 God has declared that His Word will endure forever.

(1) **First Peter 1:22-25 points out that creation is fading, but God's Word is enduring. Describe a time when you thought something you heard or read would change your life, but it ultimately fell short.**

I thought that if I became friends with this one girl that everything would change. But that didn't happen.

Scripture is eternal because its author is eternal. Human messages are temporary because people are temporary. Because God exists in eternity, His message is true at all times and in all places. God's Word is never vulnerable to relativism. It is simply not within God's nature to declare something that is true today and untrue tomorrow.

Psalm 119:89

"LORD, Your word is forever; it is firmly fixed in heaven."

(2) **Read the following verses from Psalm 119 and identify the ways they describe the eternal nature of God's Word.**
Verse 89: forever, it is firmly fixed in heaven
Verse 152: You have established them forever
Verse 160: Truth

Psalm 119:152

"Long ago I learned from Your decrees that You have established them forever."

Scripture is eternal because it gives insight into eternal issues—God's character and kingdom. We are accustomed to temporary information. The news of today, whether good or bad, is generally forgotten in less than a week. Records are broken, and this year's accomplishments are replaced by new ones next year. Trophies awarded today are quickly shelved to begin earning the next ones.

Psalm 119:160

"The entirety of Your word is truth, and all Your righteous judgments endure forever."

In contrast, God's Word addresses matters of ultimate importance—God's purposes, ways, and will for our lives. The Bible has spoken about every good deed we should do and every bad deed we should avoid. We can trust God's Word to give us direction about all of the things that really matter for this life and the next.

Read Psalm 139:17 in the margin. God's thoughts are vast. He has given us the Bible so that we can discover His eternal truth for any issue in life.

Psalm 139:17
"God, how difficult Your thoughts are for me to comprehend; how vast their sum is!"

(3) **Check some areas of your life in which you need to discover and apply the eternal truth of Scripture.**
- ☑ Knowing God's will
- ☑ Relating to others
- ☑ Growing in Christlikeness
- ☑ Making a decision
- ○ Other: _____
- ☑ Dealing with temptation
- ☑ Handling family problems
- ☑ Discovering a channel for ministry
- ☑ Overcoming a stronghold

Jesus knew He could rely on messages from His Father. When Jesus was being questioned by the **Pharisees*** about the validity of His testimony, He relied on His Father's truthfulness, saying, "I have many things to say and to judge about you, but the One who sent Me is true, and what I have heard from Him—these things I tell the world" (John 8:26).

* *Pharisees:* an ancient Jewish sect characterized by a strict observance of Old Testament laws and the Mishnah (interpretations of the law). Jesus criticized the Pharisees because of their hypocrisy.

(4) **In activity 1 you described a time when a human message fell short of changing your life. Now describe a time when the truth of God's Word made a radical difference in your life.**

When I was lost I didn't understand I looked up John 3:16. And I sorta understood a little more.

In Psalm 119:144 the singer says,

Your decrees are righteous forever.
Give me understanding, and I will live.

Pray and thank God for His enduring Word that has so richly blessed your life.

(5) **Try writing this week's memory verse in the margin.**

How I love your teaching! It is my meditation All day long Psalms 119:97

Day 4 • Trustworthy in Every Way

Read and meditate on "God's Word for Today" in the margin.
Spend a moment in prayer as you begin today's lesson.

Have you ever done a trust fall? In this exercise you stand with your back at the edge of a short platform. Meanwhile, your coworkers stand below in two lines with their arms outstretched. Then you simply fall back with the hope that they will catch you. Sounds simple—until you're on the platform.

① **Whom do you trust completely?** *Jane Elizabeth*
Why? *She's never told any of my secrets.*
Godly, Kind, Funny, Shares same intrest as me.

We should feel the freedom to fall into the care of the Bible without any worry. Why? Because the Author is perfect and will not fail to tell the truth. "God's Word for Today" comes from a song of praise by King David in 2 Samuel 22 (repeated in Psalm 18). David sang it near the end of his life in response to God's delivery of Israel from its enemies.

We can have the same response as King David because we have also received God's Word and have also found it trustworthy. Although David had only part of God's Word, we can rejoice that we have both the Old and New Testaments—God's complete written revelation.

The Bible is inerrant. Inerrancy * is the theological term used to describe the Bible's truthfulness. To state it simply, the Bible contains no errors in anything it says or affirms. We can fully trust in the Bible because of God's reliability. Titus 1:2 and Hebrews 6:18 teach that God cannot lie. Therefore, what He has revealed in the Bible is utterly trustworthy.

Inerrancy: a doctrine stating that the Bible is completely true in all it states and affirms in its original manuscripts

Titus 1:2
"... God, who cannot lie ..."

Hebrews 6:18
"It is impossible for God to lie."

② **What circumstance are you currently facing for which you need God's perfect guidance?**
Getting the word about God out.

The Bible is reliable. Yesterday you read about Jesus' interaction with the Pharisees. This religious group had felt it necessary to create the Mishnah in order to help people obey the Scriptures. The Mishnah was a collection of rabbinic interpretations of the Old Testament law. However, the Pharisees came to give the Mishnah the same authority as the law. Thus, people began to follow the words of the rabbis rather than the words of God.

3. **Check any substitutes used today for the inerrant truth of the Bible.**
   - ☑ Books
   - ☑ Magazines
   - ☑ Personal opinion
   - ☑ Experiences
   - ☑ Media
   - ☑ Politicians
   - ☑ Pop-culture personalities
   - ☑ Pastors and Bible teachers
   - ○ Other: _____

We can rely on God's Word because it speaks to both the course-altering and the minor issues of life. When God speaks, He is both true and trustworthy. The Bible provides the instruction we need to follow God faithfully.

The Bible is sufficient. God's Word contains everything we need to know in order to relate to God and live abundant, godly lives. The Bible provides guidance for every decision, temptation, and victory we will face in life. We don't need any instructions for living that the world has to offer; all we need is God's revelation in Scripture.

This truth brings us great freedom. We don't have to fear that God has withheld important information we need for relating to Him. We can also live with courage that nothing new will arise that will require God to supplement His Word. Instead, the Bible is sufficient to fully equip believers to live rightly related to the Lord and to experience the full joy of His salvation (see Deuteronomy 29:29).

Read Proverbs 30:5-6 in the margin and note God's strict command that we should not alter His Word. In Revelation God says if anyone removes any words of His prophecies, He will "take away his share of the tree of life and the holy city" (22:19). God is clear: His Word is reliable and sufficient because it is inerrant. It is inerrant because its Author is perfect.

4. **Think about the circumstance you listed in activity 2. Note ways the following characteristics of God's Word will change the way you approach this problem.**
   Inerrant: _____
   Reliable: _____
   Sufficient: _____

We don't need any instructions for living that the world has to offer; all we need is God's revelation in Scripture.

Deuteronomy 29:29
"The hidden things belong to the LORD our God, but the revealed things belong to us and our children forever, so that we may follow all the words of this law."

Proverbs 30:5-6
"Every word of God is pure; He is a shield to those who take refuge in Him. Don't add to His words, or He will rebuke you, and you will be proved a liar."

Day 5 • Loving the Author

Read and meditate on "God's Word for Today" in the margin. Spend a moment in prayer as you begin today's lesson.

My favorite book as a child was *The Call of the Wild* by Jack London. The story of Buck's unbreakable spirit in the Alaskan Klondike captivated me for hours. Though I adored the book then, I remember little of it now. It was fun to read as a child, but it had very little lasting impact on my life.

However, another piece of literature did. It was a note my mother sent to me when I was 17 years old. During the summer I served as the leader of a group of boys who went camping for a week away from their parents. The hidden note in my pack was about my mom's love and pride that her little boy was growing into a young man. Mom's letter will never be considered a classic on the level of *The Call of the Wild*, but in my life it far surpasses London's soaring literature. Why? Because I didn't know London, and I knew Mom. I'm sure London would have been a decent friend, but I loved my mother!

1) **Name an important book or correspondence you have received and indicate why it meant so much to you.**

The Bible. Because it teaches me how to live my live through him correctly.

Because God's Word is the revelation of God's heart and character, we love its message. However, we must not worship the Bible as if it were God. The Bible is not God, just as the words you speak are not you.

God authoritatively shows us through Scripture why we are to love Him.

2) **Read Psalm 119:130-131. Underline two reasons we are to love God.**

We love God for using His Word to change us. Psalm 119 is a song of praise to God for blessing us with Holy Scripture. Verses 130-131 give us one of the many reasons we are to love the Author above the Word: God's declarations bring about blessed change in our lives. We would be foolish to trust in the announcement of a blessing rather than the One who blesses us.

God's Word for Today

"How happy is the man who does not follow the advice of the wicked, or take the path of sinners, or join a group of mockers! Instead, his delight is in the LORD's instruction, and he meditates on it day and night." Psalm 1:1-2

Psalm 119:130-131

"The revelation of Your words brings light and gives understanding to the inexperienced. I pant with open mouth because I long for Your commands."

Patrick Henry, a central figure in the American Revolution, is traditionally attributed with the words "The Bible is worth all other books which have ever been printed."[1]

3) **What is your favorite Bible verse or account?** _John 3:16-17_

_____

What does it reveal about God's character or activity? _That he is eternally loving. And hes is forgiving and he gives/has one and only son_

4) **Examine "Outline of the Bible" on page 94 to discover the vast amount of direction God has generously provided in His Word to teach us and to transform our lives.** ✓

We love God for using His Word to teach us about ourselves. As a church planter in a metropolitan city, I interacted with scores of people whose religious beliefs were summed up in two statements: "I'm OK with God. God is OK with me." However, God's Word reveals an utterly different reality. In the Bible we learn that we are not OK with God, and He is not OK with us. Romans 5:10 teaches that we are God's enemies prior to being spiritually transformed by Christ. If we didn't have God's Word to show us the truth of our spiritual condition, we would blissfully skip through life ignorant of the horrible fate awaiting us after death. In addition, His Word clearly reveals how we can be reconciled with Him. When we realize God's kindness in disclosing the truth to us, we love Him even more.

The Bible is God's Word, not a word about God. Our love must be firmly planted in the conviction that God speaks through His Word and that we can love Him in response to what He says. "God's Word for Today," Psalm 1:1-2, says we can receive the instruction of the Word with delight.

Our level of appreciation for God's Word reveals something significant about our level of commitment to God Himself. Conclude your time today with prayer, asking the Lord to increase your love for Him as you spend time in His Word.

5) **Write this week's memory verse.** _How I love your teaching! It is my meditation all day long. Psalm 119:97_

"The Bible is worth all other books which have ever been printed."

Romans 5:10
"If, while we were enemies, we were reconciled to God through the death of His Son, then how much more, having been reconciled, will we be saved by His life!"

1. Henry Haley, *Haley's Bible Handbook* [online], 1965 [cited 4 February 2009]. Available from the Internet: *www.bible-history.com*.

Session 1 • Treasuring the Word

WELCOME AND PRAYER

Welcome participants and pray for God's guidance during the discussion.

OPENING ACTIVITY

1. Invite a volunteer to recite this week's memory verse.
2. Books often play an important role in shaping our lives. What was your favorite book as a child? What is your favorite book now? Why do you enjoy it so much?

REVIEW OF DAILY WORK

1. Although the Bible is the best-selling book in history, opinions about it vary. How does the world view the Bible? Do unbelievers see it as a collection of fairy tales, an imperfect collection of religious teachings, a perfect reflection of God's will, or God's revelation of Himself to humanity?
2. Before you became a Christian, how did you view the Bible? Now that you are a follower of Christ, how have your thoughts about the Bible changed?
3. Think about this week's memory verse. How does a love for God's Word affect the way we live?
4. Read Psalm 19:7-11. Discuss the benefits offered to someone who diligently follows the Scriptures.

GROUP DISCUSSION

Discover

1. Define *inerrancy* (p. 18). Why does it matter that the Bible does not have any errors? How does that knowledge change the way you respond to the Scriptures?
2. Our belief in the Bible's claim of inerrancy is based on the character of its Author. How is God's character communicated through His Word?
3. What characteristics of the Bible make it worth following? What does it claim to be that sets it apart from other religious and philosophical books?

Connect

1. Read 2 Timothy 3:16. Discuss what you learned about the phrase "inspired by God" as you studied this passage.
2. How would the human race be different if we did not have the Bible? How would your life be different if you did not have the Bible?

Relate

Read Psalm 1:1-2 and discuss the two different paths that are available to us.

Confront

1. In day 4 you learned that the Bible is reliable and sufficient. Describe a situation in your life when you need the Scriptures' help to make a decision.
2. As you continue in this study, what changes would you like to see in your life? In your study habits? In your understanding of the Bible?

Change

1. People spend time on the things they love. What people and things usually consume your time?
2. Discuss ways you will increase your time with God's Word.

MISSIONAL APPLICATION

What are specific ideas or stories in God's Word that you hope to gain a better grasp of because of this study?

PREVIEW WEEK 2

Turn to page 25 and preview the study for the coming week.

PRAYING TOGETHER

Close the session in prayer for one another.

Week 2
The Authority
of God's Word

"My word that comes from My mouth
will not return to Me empty, but it
will accomplish what I please, and will
prosper in what I send it to do."
Isaiah 55:11

The Authority of God's Word

Power has a multitude of uses. Some parents use it to generously reward their children for good grades. Some bosses use it to belittle their employees when a project has failed. Spouses use it for good or evil in marriage. Nations hold the power of their armies over one another to gain land and money.

God is different. He knows His great power can grant life or quench it. Fortunately for us, God has chosen to provide life, knowing that we cannot find it on our own. In His Word we find God's intentions perfectly and personally communicated to us.

This week's devotionals and discussions will center on the display and work of God's authority through His Word. I hope you will not just learn about His authority this week but also renew your desire to embrace the life-giving power of His Word.

OVERVIEW OF WEEK 2
Day 1: God's Power Displayed
Day 2: The Call to Salvation
Day 3: Uncovering What Is Hidden
Day 4: Our Weapon in Battle
Day 5: God's Word: Our Authority

VERSE TO MEMORIZE
"My word that comes from My mouth will not return to Me empty, but it will accomplish what I please, and will prosper in what I send it to do" (Isaiah 55:11).

DISCIPLESHIP HELPS FOR WEEK 2
"Spiritual Battle Plan" (p. 95)
"Guidelines for a Quiet Time" (p. 96)

Day 1 • God's Power Displayed

· · · · · · · · · · · · · · · · · · ·

God's Word for Today

"My word that comes from My mouth will not return to Me empty, but it will accomplish what I please, and will prosper in what I send it to do."
Isaiah 55:11

Read and meditate on "God's Word for Today" (this week's verse to memorize) in the margin. Spend a moment in prayer as you begin today's lesson. Remove the Scripture-memory card for week 2 from the back of your book and begin committing this verse to memory.

1. How empowered do you feel in the following circumstances? Circle the number that is appropriate for each area, with 5 being the greatest.

Marriage	1 2 3 4 5
Parenting	1 2 3 4 5
Staff meetings at work	1 2 3 4 5
Social gatherings	1 2 3 4 5
Current project at work	1 2 3 4 5
Personal walk with Christ	1 2 3 4 5
As a leader at church	1 2 3 4 5
Witnessing to friends	1 2 3 4 5
Spiritual warfare	1 2 3 4 5

God's Word has a great deal to teach us about every aspect of our lives. According to 2 Timothy 3:17, the Bible can prepare us for every circumstance and relationship.

2 Timothy 3:17
"… so that the man of God may be complete, equipped for every good work."

As we learned last week, God communicates His power through His Word. The Bible describes God's power and calls us to live under it. But sometimes we are slow to respond. This slowness could be due to many reasons, ranging from simply not knowing God's Word to sinful pride. Whatever the reason, this week's study is an opportunity for you to place your life fully under the power of God and His Word.

2. **What would you say is the primary reason you do not consistently live in God's power?**
   ○ Lack of knowledge of God's Word   ○ Disobedience
   ○ Not being filled with the Spirit   ○ Pride
   ○ Other: _____

God's Word is not mere philosophy that only works in a few specific life circumstances. It is at work pervasively throughout the world and our lives.

God's Word is not mere philosophy that works only in a few specific circumstances. It is at work pervasively throughout the world and our lives.

The Book of Isaiah gives a beautiful depiction of God's power at work in the world through His Word. The Old Testament prophet Isaiah was to tell the Israelites that God would deliver them but only after He had purified them. At the end of the second section of the book, God declared through Isaiah the power of His Word.

(3) **Read Isaiah 55:8-11 in the margin and fill in the blanks.**
God's thoughts are _____ than our thoughts.
God's ways are _____ than our ways.
God's Word always _____ its purpose.

God's thoughts are higher than our thoughts. Humanity makes new discoveries each day about our world, but we are unable to understand God's thoughts unless He reveals them to us. Scripture tells us that God reveals great thoughts to us through His Word (see Amos 4:13). By knowing His thoughts, we gain a powerful understanding of God's purpose for our lives.

God's ways are greater than our ways. The way God works is nobler than our pedestrian living. It is critical for followers of Christ to know how to participate in the work of God's kingdom. As God reveals His ways to us through His Word, we can join His current work in the world.

God's Word always accomplishes its purpose. Major-league baseball players practice batting hundreds of times a week. Yet a batter who hits the ball only 40 percent of the time is considered one of the greats of the game. In contrast, God never makes a vain attempt at what He sets out to do. He is perfect in all of His work, and His Word accomplishes His will.

(4) **List three important areas of your life in which you need to apply God's Word in order to experience His power.**
1. _____ 2. _____ 3. _____

Paul concluded his prayer for the Ephesian church, "Now to Him who is able to do above and beyond all that we ask or think ..." (Ephesians 3:20). Take time today to search the Scriptures for the answers to the problems you have listed. Pray and ask for God's power to work in your life according to the promises in His Word. Place your faith in His ability to work beyond your imagination.

Isaiah 55:8-11

" 'My thoughts are not your thoughts, and your ways are not My ways.' This is the LORD's declaration. 'For as heaven is higher than earth, so My ways are higher than your ways, and My thoughts than your thoughts. For just as rain and snow fall from heaven, and do not return there without saturating the earth, and making it germinate and sprout, and providing seed to sow and food to eat, so My word that comes from My mouth will not return to Me empty, but it will accomplish what I please, and will prosper in what I send it to do.' "

Amos 4:13

"He is here: the One who forms the mountains, creates the wind, and reveals His thoughts to man, the One who makes the dawn out of darkness and strides on the heights of the earth. Yahweh, the God of Hosts, is His name."

Day 2 • The Call to Salvation

Read and meditate on "God's Word for Today" in the margin.

Spend a moment in prayer as you begin today's lesson.

God's Word for Today

"I am not ashamed of the gospel, because it is God's power for salvation to everyone who believes, first to the Jew, and also to the Greek."

Romans 1:16

History is divided into B.C. and A.D., with B.C. denoting the time before Christ. A.D., or *anno domini*, means *in the year of our Lord.* Every believer also has a B.C. and an A.D. Your B.C. is your life before following Christ, and your A.D. is the time since you began following Christ.

① **Check words that describe your B.C. period of life or add your own.**
   ○ Self-destructive   ○ Self-fulfilled   ○ Sinful   ○ Good
   ○ Careless   ○ Thoughtful   ○ Hopeless   ○_____
   ○ Hope-filled   ○ Unaware   ○ Searching   ○_____

It was the gospel that moved you from your B.C. to your A.D. In "God's Word for Today" Paul proclaimed his bold confidence in the power of God's message to humanity.

② **God often uses people to show us the truth of Scripture. Who were some of the people who communicated to you God's call to salvation?**

_____

Each day we are exposed to a multitude of influential people and events. Some of these influences deal with the mundane and some with the sublime. But only Scripture has the authority and ability to give us a clear picture of our relationship with God.

Romans 1:17

"In [the gospel] God's righteousness is revealed from faith to faith, just as it is written: The righteous will live by faith."

③ **In Romans 1:17 Paul explained why the gospel must be told. Read the verse in the margin and check what is revealed in the gospel.**
   ○ A lack of faith   ○ God's righteousness   ○ God's power

Paul said the gospel must be told because only in it is God's righteousness revealed. We see God's creative power on display in the created order and His image mirrored in human beings. But God has chosen the Word as the medium to reveal His righteousness. God's Word contains something found nowhere else—the gospel. In fact, God's plan to redeem you into a relationship with Him is the core message of the Bible.

In a journey through the Bible, we come to understand that God is righteous and we are not. We see our sin in comparison to God's perfection. When comparing our lives to others, we usually decide that we are OK. But when our lives are measured against the righteousness of God as revealed in the Bible, we discover an expansive gap we cannot cross.

④ **Write the references of some Bible verses and biblical stories that helped you understand your need to become a follower of Christ.**

_____

_____

God's mission includes your salvation, but it doesn't end with it. Once we become Christians, we have the task to tell others of God's Word as well. Peter, an early leader in the church, wrote about the ancient prophets who "searched and carefully investigated" the grace of God that would come through the Messiah (1 Peter 1:10). I find it fascinating that Peter taught that the prophets were not serving their own ministries but rather us!

⑤ **Read 1 Peter 1:10-12 and circle the word *you* each time it occurs.**

The message of God's Word doesn't exist merely for prophets, preachers, and professors to debate. God has sent His Word to all of us. And we are all to carry it with the authority of His Word to those around us.

Paul, like the influential friends you named in activity 2, was not ashamed of the gospel. In fact, Paul faced constant pressure to be quiet about the message of Christ. We should follow his example to share the truth with confidence in the power of God's Word.

⑥ **Write the names of at least three friends with whom you want to share the message of God's salvation.**
    1. _____ 2. _____ 3. _____

We are tempted to be ashamed of God's Word because of ridicule by the world and hypocrisy in the church. Remember that God's Word finds its power not in the end user but in its Author. You can take comfort and gain confidence that the message you communicate is God's Word of salvation.

Pray for God's power to share the gospel with the friends you listed.

> God's Word finds its power not in the end user but in its Author.

1 Peter 1:10-12
"Concerning this salvation, the prophets who prophesied about the grace that would come to you searched and carefully investigated. They inquired into what time or what circumstances the Spirit of Christ within them was indicating when He testified in advance to the messianic sufferings and the glories that would follow. It was revealed to them that they were not serving themselves but you concerning things that have now been announced to you through those who preached the gospel to you by the Holy Spirit sent from heaven. Angels desire to look into these things."

Week 2 » Day 2

Day 3 • Uncovering What Is Hidden

 Read and meditate on "God's Word for Today" in the margin. Spend a moment in prayer as you begin today's lesson.

Books come in a multitude of categories—fiction, self-help, biography, cooking, reference—and the list goes on. Some books inspire, others inform, while many simply entertain. In contrast, the Bible has power unlike any other literary work. Because the Word is inspired by God, it has the ability to draw back the veil and reveal His truth about our lives.

The writer of Hebrews tells us that God's Word is "living" (4:12). The message of Scripture is not a cookbook-like recipe for successful living. The Bible has life within its truth. It is the message and power of God, communicated in words that comfort and challenge. Scripture is not static or passive but "living and effective" (Hebrews 4:12).

1 Peter 1:23

"You have been born again—not of perishable seed but of imperishable—through the living and enduring word of God."

(1) Hebrews 4:12 describes God's Word as "living and effective." **Read 1 Peter 1:23 in the margin and underline Peter's description of God's Word.**

First Peter 1:23 calls God's Word "living and enduring." The activity of God's Word is not simply to make life tolerable or even better. It brings about new life through God's words.

As God has brought about our new lives as believers, He has authority over them as well. Often this authority is exercised through His Word. "God's Word for Today," Hebrews 4:12, states that His "two-edged sword" penetrates and divides the internal parts of our being. This image speaks of the division between soul and spirit, joints and marrow. Whether physical or spiritual, nothing is beyond the sight and rule of God.

Whether physical or spiritual, nothing is beyond the sight and rule of God.

 Facing our sinfulness is difficult because it involves the admission of wrongdoing. Are you hiding something from other people? Is there a habit or sin that you have tried to hide from God's gaze? If so, take time in prayer to confess this sin to God and to acknowledge that He has authority over this area of your life.

Recognizing God's authority can be difficult for us. By nature we are rebels and rogues. But in His grace God gives us His Word so that we can change, not only in our eternal destiny but also in our everyday living.

2. **For what reasons do you avoid placing yourself under the gaze of Scripture?**
   ○ Embarrassed by your behavior   ○ Afraid of the consequences
   ○ Ashamed of an ongoing habit   ○ Do not want to change
   ○ Disagree with the Bible's assessment of your activity

Ultimately, our attempts to hide from God and His Word are futile, for "it is a judge of the ideas and thoughts of the heart" (Hebrews 4:12). The next verse says, "No creature is hidden from Him, but all things are naked and exposed to the eyes of Him to whom we must give an account" (Hebrews 4:13). God's Word sees our lives as they truly stand. It cuts through our wasted efforts to hide and delivers truthful commentary on life.

3. **Read Jeremiah 23:29. In what way is God's Word like fire?** _____
_____

   In what way is God's Word like a sledgehammer? _____
_____

> **Jeremiah 23:29**
> " 'Is not My word like fire'—
>   the LORD's declaration—
>   'and like a sledgehammer
>   that pulverizes rock?' "

God's Word works like a fire and a sledgehammer in our lives; nothing can stand in its way. It burns through any defense and breaks down any fortress. We can't hide the details of our lives—and sins—from God.

We must also allow God's Word to be the source of conviction in other people's lives. God has not asked us to measure their lives against ours. We are to hold up God's revelation through His Word as the measuring rod for all of us. As we have spiritual conversations with friends who don't have a relationship with God, we can be confident in the power of Scripture to convict them of their need. If we truly believe it is "living and effective" (Hebrews 4:12) , we don't need to be concerned that they will not understand it. By His Spirit, God will use the fire and sledgehammer of His Word to uncover their hidden need for His transforming power.

4. **Try writing this week's memory verse in the margin. Claim this verse as you present the message of salvation to people who need Christ.**

Day 4 • Our Weapon in Battle

God's Word for Today

"Take the helmet of salvation, and the sword of the Spirit, which is God's word."
Ephesians 6:17

 Read and meditate on "God's Word for Today" in the margin. Spend a moment in prayer as you begin today's lesson.

I remember my first real fight as a boy. Another kid on the playground kept pushing me around. He thought it was funny, but I was just plain mad. And then it happened—I threw my first punch. The only problem was that I missed his chin by a mile. But by virtue of the fact that I threw a punch, he never bothered me again!

I wish our spiritual battles were as easy. Instead, our enemy comes after us day after day after day. He constantly attacks us with fiery darts of temptation and whispers thoughts of hopelessness into our lives.

① **Check any recent temptations in your life or add your own.**
- ○ Anger
- ○ Bitterness
- ○ Envy
- ○ Hopelessness
- ○ Lying
- ○ Gluttony
- ○ Worry
- ○ Drunkenness
- ○ Apathy
- ○ Idolatry
- ○ Lust
- ○ _____

Many temptations deal with physical battles, like gluttony. But all of them deal in some way with our mind and spirit. The battle we face does not occur on the earth. We are facing spiritual powers bent on our destruction.

2 Corinthians 10:3-5
"Although we are walking in the flesh, we do not wage war in a fleshly way, since the weapons of our warfare are not fleshly, but are powerful through God for the demolition of strongholds. We demolish arguments and every high-minded thing that is raised up against the knowledge of God, taking every thought captive to the obedience of Christ."

② **Read 2 Corinthians 10:3-5 in the margin. How do we wage spiritual warfare?**

_____

_____

These verses state that we fight with weapons that are not made on earth. Because we face spiritual battles, we must fight with spiritual weapons.

③ **Read Ephesians 6:11-18 in the margin on page 33. Write *O* beside the armor that is offensive and *D* beside the armor that is defensive.**
- ___ Belt of truth
- ___ Armor of righteousness
- ___ Shoes of peace
- ___ Shield of faith
- ___ Helmet of salvation
- ___ Sword of the Spirit

The sword of the Spirit—the Word of God—is the only offensive weapon in the spiritual armor. In the same passage Paul also gave several commands we need to follow while on the battlefield:
• "Stand against the tactics of the Devil" (v. 11).
• "Resist in the evil day" (v. 13).
• "Take your stand" (v. 13).

God doesn't wants us to run away from battle when we are tempted. Rather, He has provided us with the one weapon that can deliver victory— His Word. When we wield the Word of God on the battlefield, we don't use our own strength or intelligence. The sword of the Spirit comes with its own power, and it never needs sharpening. We use it by simply speaking what God has already said and by trusting in what God has already declared as true.

Conventional warfare provides some lessons for using the sword of the Spirit in warfare. Soldiers are taught how to care for and use their weapons in every possible scenario. In some cases they learn how to disassemble and reassemble a rifle while blindfolded. What is the purpose of such an exercise? To know every facet of the weapon so intimately that by merely touching a part, they recognize its place and use.

④ **How well do you know the sword of the Spirit—the Word of God? Check the skills you have acquired.**
○ I have memorized the names and order of the books of the Bible.
○ I understand the basic storyline of the Old Testament.
○ I understand the basic storyline of the New Testament.
○ I can explain the gospel to a lost person.
○ I have memorized Scripture passages to overcome temptation.
○ I understand how to interpret a passage of Scripture.

Knowing how to use the Word of God is vital to our ability to stand against our spiritual enemy. As you move through this study, I hope you will commit to become a better student of the Bible and therefore a better soldier in using the sword of the Spirit.

⑤ **Turn to "Spiritual Battle Plan" on page 95 and discover ways you can use God's Word in everyday events and temptations.**

Ephesians 6:11-18
"Put on the full armor of God so that you can stand against the tactics of the Devil. For our battle is not against flesh and blood, but against the rulers, against the authorities, against the world powers of this darkness, against the spiritual forces of evil in the heavens. This is why you must take up the full armor of God, so that you may be able to resist in the evil day, and having prepared everything, to take your stand. Stand, therefore, with truth like a belt around your waist, righteousness like armor on your chest, and your feet sandaled with readiness for the gospel of peace. In every situation take the shield of faith, and with it you will be able to extinguish the flaming arrows of the evil one. Take the helmet of salvation, and the sword of the Spirit, which is God's word. With every prayer and request, pray at all times in the Spirit, and stay alert in this, with all perseverance and intercession for all the saints."

Day 5 • God's Word: Our Authority

Read and meditate on "God's Word for Today" in the margin.
Spend a moment in prayer as you begin today's lesson.

God's Word for Today

"I delight to do Your will, my God; Your instruction resides within me." Psalm 40:8

God has not asked you to establish a treaty with Him. Rather, He requires absolute surrender. A treaty means that two separate countries retain their own boundaries, sovereignty, and trade favors with each other. A surrender means that one country comes under the authority of another. God is not One with whom we bargain. He authoritatively speaks about His character and will. We are called to surrender, not barter for favors.

1. **Beside each action write** *T* **for a** *treaty* **or** *S* **for** *surrender.*
   ___ Keep authority over my life
   ___ Serve another king
   ___ Trade favors with another power
   ___ Follow another's directives

Henry Blackaby uses the phrase "unhurried time with God" to describe the way we should regard our time with God's Word.[1] The phrase describes a perspective of heart that enjoys time spent with God in Scripture and prayer. In many cases we have allowed our daily schedules to dictate how much time we give to God's Word. Instead, we should commit to a regular time with God and then remain in study and prayer until we have learned what God desires to teach us.

> We should commit to a regular time with God and then remain in study and prayer until we have learned what God desires to teach us.

To hold such an attitude requires a shift of power in our lives. We must give up the throne and allow Christ to sit in His rightful place. This is not an ethereal notion. Either Jesus is Lord, or He is not. When Christ rules our lives, He must reign over every aspect—including our daily schedules, the devotion of our hearts, and the attention of our minds.

2. **Do you keep a regular quiet time in prayer and Bible study?**
   ○ Yes ○ No

   If not, what seems to be the major barrier to a regular time with God?
   ○ Hurry ○ Other priorities ○ Never thought about a quiet time
   ○ Other: _____

Unfortunately, most of us see hurry and rush as the norms for our lives. A life dedicated to the close study of God's Word requires stillness, quiet, and submission. To make God's Word the authority in our spiritual journeys, we must remove the barriers of hurry and worry (see Psalm 46:10).

Related to these barriers is our need to know what is next. Often we feel either self-assured that we know what is going to happen next or utterly hopeless that we don't have a clue what's next. Bringing our lives under the authority of God's Word lifts the burden of needing to be in control of the next thing. God's Word teaches that worry has no place in a believer's life; instead, we are to trust in God.

In Matthew 6:25-34 Jesus taught us to take a lesson from the flowers of the field and the birds of the air instead of worrying about what is next. Just as nature simply lives in God's grace, believers have access to the revelation of God's grace through His Word. When we read God's Word each day, we can choose simply to trust in how God is equipping us for the day ahead through the transforming power of His Word.

An African-American pastor once began his sermon by saying, "Yes, Lord." He repeated these words over and over until the congregation began to say them with him, "Yes, Lord. Yes, Lord. Yes. Lord." After several minutes the pastor stopped, and so did the congregation. Once it was quiet, the pastor simply said, "Lord, You've heard our answer. Now what's Your request?"

We should develop the habit of saying yes to all of God's Word, rejoicing in the opportunity to follow our King. God's Word has power, it is living, and it is our weapon in battle. Say yes to every request God makes of you and rejoice in every revelation of His Word.

③ **Turn to page 96 and read "Guidelines for a Quiet Time." Make notes in the margin of that page about having regular time alone with God.**

Spend time in prayer saying yes to God's authority in your life through His Word. Make any commitment He is leading you to make about a regular quiet time and about trusting in the authority of His Word.

④ **Write this week's memory verse in the margin.**

Psalm 46:10
"Stop your fighting—
and know that I am God,
exalted among the nations,
exalted on the earth."

Bringing our lives under the authority of God's Word lifts the burden of needing to be in control of the next thing.

Week 2 » Day 5

1. Doy Cave, "God Misses You Too," *Christian Single* [online, cited 11 February 2009]. Available from the Internet: *www.lifeway.com*.

Session 2 • The Authority of God's Word

WELCOME AND PRAYER

OPENING ACTIVITY
1. Invite a participant to recite this week's memory verse.
2. Identify the person who you think has the most authority or power in the world today.

REVIEW OF DAILY WORK
1. Share responses to activity 4 on page 27.
2. Share responses to activity 4 on page 29.

GROUP DISCUSSION

Discover
1. How did your study of the power of God's Word affect your view of the Bible?
2. Read aloud Isaiah 55:8-11. Describe a time when read a verse and then saw its truth come to pass in your life.
3. How have you seen God's Word at work in your life or in the life of your family?

Connect
1. Name words the Bible uses to describe our lives prior to salvation.
2. What biblical stories or passages were key to your understanding the need to have a relationship with Christ?
3. What are some of your favorite Bible verses or passages today?

Relate
1. Ephesians 6:11-18 describes the spiritual armor. What are some circumstances in which you need to use the sword of the Spirit?
2. Discuss what these statements teach about wielding the sword of the Spirit: "The sword of the Spirit comes with its own power, and it never needs sharpening. We use it by simply speaking what God has already said and by trusting in what God has already declared as true" (p. 33).
3. Which of the following words would you use to describe your experience of studying the power of God's Word this week?

○ Convicting   ○ Joyful   ○ Challenging   ○ Liberating
○ Time-consuming   ○ Hard   ○ Frustrating   ○ Embarrassing
○ Enlightening   ○ Easy   ○ Other: _____
Explain why you chose that word.

Confront

1. Jeremiah 23:29 says, " 'Is not My word like fire'—the LORD's declaration—'and like a sledgehammer that pulverizes rock?' " What can God's Word do to strongholds of sin in our lives?
2. Discuss responses to exercise 3 on page 32.

Change

1. How is your view of God's Word changing through this study?
2. What commitment did you make this week to study God's Word regularly and to trust the authority of God's Word (prayer activity, p. 35)?

MISSIONAL APPLICATION

1. God's Word leads us to understand our lives from God's perspective. How are your ideas and thoughts about the following areas changing as you grow in your commitment to live God's Word?
   • Work
   • Marriage and parenting
   • Social relationships
   • Worship
   • Service to others
   • Walk with Christ

2. In activity 6 on page 29 you were asked to write the names of friends with whom you hope to share the message of Christ. Share first names and pray for them.

PREVIEW WEEK 3

Turn to page 39 and preview the study for the coming week.

PRAYING TOGETHER

Close the session by praying for one another.

Transformed
by the Word

"All Scripture is inspired by God and is profitable for teaching, for rebuking, for correcting, for
training in righteousness, so that the man of God
may be complete, equipped for every good work."

2 Timothy 3:16–17

Transformed by the Word

As a little boy, I was obsessed with "Transformers," a cartoon about alien robots that could transform themselves into various vehicles and other mechanical objects. The good guys were the Autobots, and the villains were the Decepticons. Every week mundane objects like cars and planes became powerful robots that battled to save or enslave the earth.

Now that I am grown, I indulge my childish fascination with "Transformers" only when my two sons are around. But secretly—don't tell anyone—I still really like it. The thought that at any moment someone could change into something completely different is pretty cool.

For a Christian, transformation is not fiction. It is anchored in the reality of God and the redemptive work accomplished by Christ. This week we will focus on 2 Timothy 3:16-17 to learn how God's Word brings about transformation in our lives.

OVERVIEW OF WEEK 3
Day 1: Teaching
Day 2: Rebuking
Day 3: Correcting
Day 4: Training
Day 5: Equipped for Every Good Work

VERSES TO MEMORIZE
"All Scripture is inspired by God and is profitable for teaching, for rebuking, for correcting, for training in righteousness, so that the man of God may be complete, equipped for every good work" (2 Timothy 3:16-17).

DISCIPLESHIP HELPS FOR WEEK 3
"Key Doctrines of the Bible" (p. 97)
"Lead Subject of Each Bible Book" (p. 98)

Day 1 • Teaching

Read and meditate on "God's Word for Today" (this week's verse to memorize) in the margin. Spend a moment in prayer as you begin today's lesson. Remove the Scripture-memory card for week 3 from the back of your book and begin committing these verses to memory.

God's Word for Today

"All Scripture is inspired by God and is profitable for teaching, for rebuking, for correcting, for training in righteousness, so that the man of God may be complete, equipped for every good work."
2 Timothy 3:16-17

When we were in school, certain subjects often became our favorites because of great teachers who were able to inspire us with the their love for the subject matter. They brought life to what seemed to be a lifeless subject.

1. What was your favorite subject when you were in school as a child? What made it fascinating to you?

We are learning that God's Word is not passive. It is active, and its activity changes our very nature. As we move from being an enemy of God's kingdom to being a friend of the King, we must learn a new way of living. God's Word serves as a teacher for this new life.

God's Word serves as a teacher for this new life.

The New Testament was written using *koine* (or common) Greek. In 2 Timothy 3:16 the word used for *teaching* is *didaskalia*. Of the 21 times it is used in the New Testament, 15 are in Paul's **pastoral epistles.*** The apostle Paul used this word to specifically designate a type of teaching with divine authority behind it. So what does God want to teach us through the Scriptures?

God uses His Word to teach us about Himself. We have already learned that God's Word is a self-revelation. Through divinely inspired writers God teaches us about His own character.

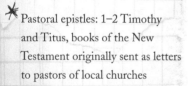

*Pastoral epistles: 1–2 Timothy and Titus, books of the New Testament originally sent as letters to pastors of local churches

The Old Testament prophet Isaiah was assigned the unenviable task of delivering God's message of judgment to the people of Israel. God hoped to call the Hebrew nation back to a faithful relationship with Him. But they needed to understand the greatness of the One they had offended with their sin. In chapter 57 God once again decried the practices of false religion and offered a portrait of Himself to which His people could cling.

② Read Isaiah 57:15 in the margin. What quality does this verse reveal about God? _____ Underline in the verse the two types of people with whom God will relate.

God taught that by His nature He is holy and high above all humanity. But He also taught us that He is willing to be friends with people who are humble and penitent. In His Word God teaches us about His character so that we can learn how to honor and relate to Him.

God uses His Word to teach us how to live. A common question I have been asked as a pastor is "What should I do next?" At the heart of that question is the desire to act properly. When we see Christ's life illustrated in Scripture, we want to imitate it. And we should. God uses His Word to teach us how to become like His Son. Scripture presents us with no higher goal than to be like Jesus.

Several books in the Bible are structured to teach us about God first and then how we are to live. For example, the Book of Romans teaches about the nature of God and salvation in chapters 1–11. Then chapters 12–16 teach us how this knowledge should cause us to live.

First Peter 1:14-16 teaches us that our conduct depends on whom we know: "As the One who called you is holy, you also are to be holy in your conduct." As we learn more of God, we will also learn how we are to live before Him.

③ What is the latest truth God has taught you through His Word?

_____

God uses His Word to teach us how to relate to others. Even a superficial reading of the Bible reveals the importance God gives to relationships. For example, He placed a man and a woman in the garden of Eden. He created the nation of Israel to be the people of God. Jesus called 12 men to be His disciples. The original Greek word for *church* refers to a collection of people.

④ Read the verses in the margin and write the phrase that is repeated.

_____

God intends for us to live in relationships with *one another*. His Word shows us how to live properly in all of our relationships.

Isaiah 57:15
"The High and Exalted One who lives forever, whose name is Holy says this: 'I live in a high and holy place, and with the oppressed and lowly of spirit, to revive the spirit of the lowly and revive the heart of the oppressed.' "

John 13:34
"I give you a new commandment: love one another. Just as I have loved you, you must also love one another."

Romans 12:16
"Be in agreement with one another."

Galatians 6:2
"Carry one another's burdens; in this way you will fulfill the law of Christ."

Ephesians 5:21
"… submitting to one another in the fear of Christ."

1 Peter 4:9
"Be hospitable to one another without complaining."

Day 2 • Rebuking

↕ **Read and meditate on "God's Word for Today" in the margin.**
Spend a moment in prayer as you being today's lesson.

The sound of today's title does not sound pleasant at all—*rebuking*.
Just pronouncing it carries an ominous tone.

① **What image comes to mind when you hear the word *rebuke*?**

_____

The word *rebuke* might evoke images of disapproval and harshness. However,
our Scripture-memory verses for this week, 2 Timothy 3:16-17, identify
rebuke as an important function of Scripture. As Paul gave instructions
to the pastor Timothy, he taught him that God's Word has the power to
rebuke believers. The young pastor must have been relieved to know that
the job of rebuking didn't fall on him but on God's Word.

Today we can also be relieved that God redirects our lives through His
Word. The word *rebuke* means to be shown our sin and hear the call to
change our behavior. It carries connotations that are important for us
to discern as we interact with God's Word.

Rebuke convicts us of sin. Only God's Word can teach us the difference
between right and wrong. Once we know that, Scripture also motivates us
to do what is right. As we spend time in the Word, it brings rebuke when
we sin. In essence, Scripture tells us to stop what we are doing wrong.

② **Beside the stop sign write an action God has recently convicted you
to stop. You may want to use abbreviations to maintain privacy.**

Before God we are like children. When children see an electrical socket,
they might not see danger but a hole that needs to be filled with something

metal. One job of a parent is to show children their errors so that they can learn safe and responsible behavior. Similarly, when we sin, only God is able to recognize the danger inherent in our actions outside His truth. That truth is revealed in His Word.

Rebuke exposes the truth. As God's Word rebukes us, it also exposes the truth of how we are living. Last week we learned from Hebrews 4:12 the power of God's Word to uncover the hidden parts of our lives. His Word shows us the thoughts and actions that are just and right in His sight. The Bible uncovers the deepest secrets we seek to hide from God. We can't hide anything from the One who knows all things.

Hebrews 4:12
"The word of God is living and effective and sharper than any two-edged sword, penetrating as far as to divide soul, spirit, joints, and marrow; it is a judge of the ideas and thoughts of the heart."

③ **What are the ways you seek to avoid the truth about your sin?**
   ⊘ Avoid Bible passages about it   ⊘ Tune out sermons about it
   ⊘ Quit praying about it   ⊘ Rationalize it
   ○ Other: _____

   How do you respond when God's Word convicts you about sin?
   ○ Repent and change the behavior   ○ Continue the behavior

Occasionally, unbelievers say they think God is portrayed as cruel in the Bible, a fierce Deity raining down fire and judgment on people. Certainly, God punishes sin without hesitation or reservation. But His intent is to reveal our sin so that we can repent and ask God to restore our relationship with Him. When we learn the truth in His Word, our responsibility is to align our hearts and minds with that truth and to adjust our behavior accordingly. That is the goal of biblical rebuke.

Through the Old Testament prophet Isaiah, God delivered devastating messages to Israel because of its sin. He allowed calamity to fall on the nation because of its idolatry. But He also offered hope of a renewed relationship. Isaiah 44:22 says God wants to sweep away our sin as the sun burns away the morning mist. God's Word can bring strong rebuke, but its goal is always redemptive. In the Bible the repentant always find new hope.

Isaiah 44:22
"I have swept away your transgressions like a cloud, and your sins like a mist. Return to Me, for I have redeemed you."

We all hold on to certain sins as if they will not truly harm us, but all sin damages our relationship with our Heavenly Father. Conclude your devotional time today with prayer. Ask God to bring Scriptures to your memory that will rebuke you for sin and lead you back to Him.

Day 3 • Correcting

God's Word for Today

"No discipline seems enjoyable at the time, but painful. Later on, however, it yields the fruit of peace and righteousness to those who have been trained by it." Hebrews 12:11

God wants our lives to align with His will and His purposes.

Read and meditate on "God's Word for Today" in the margin.
Spend a moment in prayer as you being today's lesson.

Yesterday I was in a huge hurry as I drove home. Quickly changing lanes, I darted in and out of traffic. As I started to zip into another lane on the interstate, the corrective honk of a car horn filled my ears. I was about to make a terrible mistake by crashing into someone's car. The blast of that car horn changed my driving and saved me from a potential tragedy.

1. **How do you respond when someone tries to correct your behavior?**
   ○ Tell them to mind their own business
   ○ Submit to correction if it aligns with God's Word
   ○ Other: _____

In 2 Timothy 3:16-17 Paul wrote that God's inspired Word has the power to correct us. The Greek word used by Paul literally means "a restoration to an upright or right state."[1] The intent of Scripture is not for us to reach a morally neutral position. Rather, God seeks to change the way we live. God wants our lives to align with His will and His purposes. One way He does that is to bring correction as we read and apply Scripture.

2. **Refer to "God's Word for Today," Hebrews 12:11, as you answer these questions.**
   How is discipline described? _____

   _____

   What does discipline yield? _____

   _____

Discipline is not pleasant. In fact, it seems painful at the time. It brings about sorrow, whether for a child who has misbehaved, a teen who has to be grounded, or an adult who has broken the law. God's correction of our lives is no different. When we are corrected by His Word, our emotions range from embarrassment to frustration to remorse. But if we endure the discipline and correct our ways, our lives can exhibit the righteousness we possess through the indwelling presence of Jesus Christ.

Once we have gone through the discipline, then we reap its benefits. It is much harder to see the benefit while being disciplined. Our ego cries out to justify our actions, and our heart cries out for mercy to ignore them. But if we are to live like Jesus, as God desires, He must bring correction to our lives through His Word.

(3) Identify a Bible verse God has used to correct your behavior.

_____

God's Word corrects our actions. God's Word reveals many areas in which we need correction. It also shows us the correct path to live for His glory. The Book of Proverbs is a treasury of guidance for staying on the right path. The author of Proverbs wrote as a father to a son who needed wisdom.

(4) Read Proverbs 3:5-7 in the margin. How can we find the right path?

_____

When we learn the wisdom of God, the right actions will follow. As a pastor, I have often been asked, "What is God's will for my life?" The first answer I give is to follow God's revealed will in His Word. We should discover what He has already said to us and obey it first. If we trust God's ways, we will shun the path of evil.

God's Word restores right thinking. In Romans 12:1 Paul encouraged believers to become "living sacrifices" for God. In verse 2 he followed up that radical call with a directive to renew our thinking in order to understand God's ways. Placing ourselves under the corrective work of God's Word will often mean that we must change our minds about a subject, an action, or a person. Most often, God's correction will aid us in understanding His character more fully, bringing us to a greater commitment to aligning our hearts with His.

Pray and commit yourself to God's correction of your actions and thinking through His Word. Ask Him to transform you so that you will know how to fulfill His perfect will.

(5) Write this week's memory verses. _____

_____

_____

Proverbs 3:5-7

"Trust in the LORD with all your heart, and do not rely on your own understanding; think about Him in all your ways, and He will guide you on the right paths. Don't consider yourself to be wise; fear the LORD and turn away from evil."

Romans 12:1-2

"By the mercies of God, I urge you to present your bodies as a living sacrifice, holy and pleasing to God; this is your spiritual worship. Do not be conformed to this age, but be transformed by the renewing of your mind, so that you may discern what is the good, pleasing, and perfect will of God."

1. W. E. Vine, *Vine's Amplified Expository Dictionary of New Testament Words, Reference Edition* (Iowa Falls: World Bible Publishers), 167.

Day 4 • Training

Read and meditate on "God's Word for Today" in the margin.
Spend a moment in prayer as you begin today's lesson.

Perhaps you have heard or read the following poem.

> Sow a thought, reap an action.
> Sow an action, reap a habit.
> Sow a habit, reap a character.
> Sow a character, reap a destiny.

(1) What are some godly thoughts you are sowing in your life? How?

_____

God's Word trains us to join His work. "God's Word for Today," Deuteronomy 29:29, describes parents' teaching God's Word to their children. Being a parent myself, I am trying to learn what God wants to accomplish through me. My two sons are very different. One is loud and the other quiet; one is bold and the other shy; one loves slapstick and the other sarcasm. But I teach both to obey the same set of rules in our home. Regardless of their differences, they must be taught to obey the same set of regulations.

This goal brings to light one of the greatest differences between me as an earthly father and God, our Heavenly Father—the rules. The training I offer is earthly and pedestrian in nature. Truth be told, our house rules are often derived from the hope of simply maintaining order. On the other end of the spectrum is God, who is revealing the "hidden things" of His nature, character, and kingdom (Deuteronomy 29:29). He is training us not to merely keep humanity in a state of moral neutrality but to seek a greater purpose. God trains us to participate in His redemptive work.

(2) **What is the primary reason you think people most often obey rules?**
○ To gain rewards ◉ To avoid punishment
○ Because they love rules ◉ To please the rule giver

How is a believer's motivation to obey God's Word different?

_____

God's Word for Today

"The hidden things belong to the LORD our God, but the revealed things belong to us and our children forever, so that we may follow all the words of this law."
Deuteronomy 29:29

God trains us to participate in His redemptive work.

Deuteronomy 29:29 shows that God reveals what we need to know to follow Him in obedience. In fact, *Deuteronomy* literally means *second law*. The Hebrews' needed to understand God's law, so He revealed it to them twice. Training requires repetition. Remember going over your multiplication tables, repeating the state capitals, and poring over grammar rules in school? Yet most of us haven't spent comparable amounts of time in God's Word. Why? It is worth our time. We need the training. Our lives are better when we hear and obey it. And the ultimate goal of our training in the Word is of great importance—joining God in kingdom work.

God's Word trains us in eternal truth. Deuteronomy 29:29 assures us that the revelations of God's Word belong to us forever. The training I endure at a gym, in human-resources orientation, or at school is generally temporary in nature. The workouts have to be continued, and the education has to be enhanced. But the training we receive through God's Word is different.

③ **Read 1 Timothy 4:8 in the margin. How does training in godliness differ from training of the body?**

_____

_____

God's Word reveals eternal truth that needs no enhancement. His Word is completely sufficient to train us for living this life and the one to come.

④ **Turn to page 97 and read "Key Doctrines of the Bible." Circle one of the doctrines you would like to learn more about.**

God's Word trains us in righteousness.* Second Timothy 3:16 ends with the phrase "for training in righteousness." Our training has a point—righteous living. The purpose behind God's self-revelation in His Word is our redemption so that we can have a relationship with Him. Our righteousness, made possible only through Jesus, brings glory to God, draws people to Him, and allows us to be useful in His kingdom.

⑤ **Rank your spiritual training by marking phrases that describe you.**
   ○ Read and obey the Word   ○ Live a righteous life
   ○ Grow in Christ   ○ Participate in kingdom work

⑥ **What is one thing you will do to enhance your spiritual training?**

_____

1 Timothy 4:8
"The training of the body has a limited benefit, but godliness is beneficial in every way, since it holds promise for the present life and also for the life to come."

* Righteousness: "positive evaluation of character, actions, and attitudes in relation to God's perfect standard"[1]

1. Henry O. Holloman, *Kregel Dictionary of the Bible and Theology* (Grand Rapids: Kregel Publications, 2005), 470.

Day 5 • Equipped for Every Good Work

God's Word for Today

"If anyone purifies himself from these things, he will be a special instrument, set apart, useful to the Master, prepared for every good work."
2 Timothy 2:21

Read and meditate on "God's Word for Today" in the margin.
Spend a moment in prayer as you being today's lesson.

Henry Ward Beecher, a 19th-century minister, reportedly said, "Sink the Bible to the bottom of the ocean, and still man's obligations to God would be unchanged. He would have the same path to tread, only his lamp and guide would be gone; the same voyage to make, but his chart and compass would be overboard!"[1] Beecher knew how desperately we need God's Word to be obedient to God's will and purpose for our lives.

1. **Record this week's memory verses and then underline an important reason God gave us His Word.** _____

_____

_____

God's intention is for His Word to equip us "for every good work" (2 Timothy 3:17). God has not assigned us tasks in His kingdom without providing the means to accomplish this work. Knowing our inability to do any kingdom task without His help, God provided the Scriptures to teach, rebuke, correct, and train us for each task so that we can advance His kingdom and bring glory to Him.

2. **What do you most need from God's Word now?**
   ○ Teaching   ○ Rebuking   ○ Correcting   ○ Training

When you submit yourself to the work of God's Word, it will equip you for whatever God calls you to do.

When you submit yourself to the work of God's Word, it will equip you for whatever God calls you to do. "God's Word for Today" falls in the middle of Paul's instruction for Timothy to be faithful in his task. Many of us are thankful for encouragement, but what we truly need is assurance. Second Timothy 2:21 was Paul's reminder to Timothy—and us—that we are a "special instrument, set apart, useful to the Master, prepared for every good work." These words assure us of God's intention for our lives. We are not afterthoughts, extras, or maybes in God's kingdom. By His salvation and through the power of His Word, we are prepared for "every good work" (2 Timothy 3:17).

(3) Rank the degree to which you feel equipped to participate in the following ministries. Let *1* mean *poor* and *5* mean *great*.

Pray for a friend	1	2	3	4	5
Share the good news of Jesus	1	2	3	4	5
Explain a Bible verse	1	2	3	4	5
Serve the needy	1	2	3	4	5
Care for someone who is grieving	1	2	3	4	5
Counsel someone with a problem	1	2	3	4	5

If you feel poorly equipped, it's time to dig deeper into the Word. The Devil will tempt us to feel shame and guilt so that we avoid God's Word. God desires the exact opposite: for us to engage His Word so that we are fully prepared for worship, witnessing, and work in and through His church. God cares for you, and He has prepared His Word to equip you to carry out the work He has for you to do in His kingdom.

(4) What are some tasks or ministries you know God asked you to accomplish, but you didn't obey because you were afraid you might fail?

_____

_____

 Take time to pray for the following needs related to those tasks.
• Forgiveness for disobeying God
• Understanding of His Word in preparation for obedience
• A time in the near future to complete the work He gave you to do
• A sensitive heart that welcomes God's assignments

(5) The more thoroughly you know the Bible, the better equipped you will be to do good works. The Bible covers a multitude of subjects. Knowing the general theme of each Bible book will help you search for instruction in God's Word and guide others to God's truth for their lives. Turn to page 98 and read "Lead Subject of Each Bible Book." Take note of books you have not read and of those that would help with your current spiritual questions.

> God has prepared His Word to equip you to carry out the work He has for you to do in His kingdom.

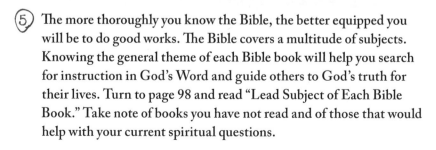

1. Alfred Armand Montapert, *Distilled Wisdom* [online], 1965 [cited 4 February 2009]. Available from the Internet: *www.hbu.edu*.

Session 3 • Transformed by the Word

WELCOME AND PRAYER

Pray for God's guidance during today's discussion.

OPENING ACTIVITY

1. Invite a participant to recite this week's memory verses.
2. Talk about your teenage years. What transformations did you go through? Was there an "ugly duckling" in your school who was transformed into a "swan"?

REVIEW OF DAILY WORK

1. Read Romans 12:1-2. God's Word reveals the character of Jesus and helps us change to be like Him. Do today's Christians need to be transformed more in their attitudes, beliefs, or actions? Why?
2. Second Timothy 3:16 states that God's Word is "profitable." What do we gain from studying the Bible?

GROUP DISCUSSION

Discover

In day 1 you learned that God's Word teaches us about three things. What are they? On which one do you currently focus most of your Bible study?

Connect

1. What is your reaction when you find something you never knew existed but you know will be very helpful? Read Deuteronomy 29:29. Describe some discoveries you have made in the Scriptures.
2. How are the truths God has revealed through Scripture enabling you to better follow His way of living?

Relate

1. Read Proverbs 3:1-7. In day 3 you read verses 5-7 and learned how God's Word corrects us. Now that you have read the rest of the passage, discuss the benefits of following God's Word, as described in verses 1-4.
2. Proverbs 3:5 tells us to trust God with our whole hearts. What are the possible results when we trust God halfheartedly? Wholeheartedly?

Confront

1. Second Timothy 3:16 uses the words *rebuking* and *correcting* to describe part of God's work through Scripture. Why is it necessary for God's Word to take these measures in our lives?

2. In what ways does God's Word rebuke us (day 2)? In what ways does God's Word correct us (day 3)?

3. What is the goal of biblical rebuke? When the teaching of Scripture rebukes you, what is your normal reaction? What does God expect you to do in response to rebuke?

4. Ask a volunteer to share a way God's Word has brought rebuke and correction in his or her life.

Change

1. Second Timothy 3:17 teaches that we are equipped for "every good work." How does God's Word prepare you for good works?

2. Share responses to activity 4 on page 49. Discuss from day 4 the ways God's Word trains us for good works. Identify opportunities for good works that are available in your church and community.

3. How has this week's study of 2 Timothy 3:16-17 challenged you to study God's Word differently?

MISSIONAL APPLICATION

1. Some people think years of studying the Bible are needed before going out and doing good things on behalf of God. What is required for a person to get ready to serve God?

2. How has this week's study of 2 Timothy 3:16-17 challenged you to participate in God's kingdom work or to train for that work?

PREVIEW WEEK 4

Turn to page 53 and preview the study for the coming week.

PRAYING TOGETHER

Close the session in prayer for one another.

Week 4

How to Study
the Word

"Help me understand
Your instruction, and
I will obey it and follow
it with all my heart."

Psalm 119:34

How to Study the Word

For me, becoming a good student was born out of necessity rather than desire. In high school I skated by, making decent grades without trying too hard; but then something happened to me—college algebra. Suddenly, I learned the real meaning of the word *study*. To learn the necessary material, I had to listen carefully, read diligently, and review often. Attempting to master algebra was humbling.

My experience with algebra illustrates the way we face life's challenges. Each day brings a new set of circumstances through which we can see God's kingdom purposes for our lives and His glory. To our great advantage, we can apply God's Word to our everyday circumstances. But to do so, we must know how to properly study and apply it.

We should approach God's Word with humility. We are inquirers rather than informers. This week you will gain some practical skills for studying God's Word. Rather than feeling overwhelmed by the "algebra" of each day, we can face our circumstances with the confidence that comes from hearing from God through His Word.

OVERVIEW OF WEEK 4
Day 1: Asking the Right Questions
Day 2: Reading for All Its Worth
Day 3: Meditating and Memorizing
Day 4: Understanding Genres
Day 5: Two Major Themes

VERSE TO MEMORIZE
"Help me understand Your instruction, and I will obey it
and follow it with all my heart" (Psalm 119:34).

DISCIPLESHIP HELPS FOR WEEK 4
"Scripture-Passage Worksheet" (p. 99)
"Bible-Study Tools" (pp. 100–101)
"Recommended Resources" (p. 102)
"Bible-Reading Plans" (p. 103)
"Tips for Memorizing Scripture" (p. 104)
"Outline of the Bible" (p. 94)

Day 1 • Asking the Right Questions

God's Word for Today

"Help me understand Your instruction, and I will obey it and follow it with all my heart." Psalm 119:34

Read and meditate on "God's Word for Today" (this week's verse to memorize) in the margin. Spend a moment in prayer as you begin today's lesson. Remove the Scripture-memory card for week 4 from the back of your book and begin committing this verse to memory.

Remember the feeling you had in school when the teacher called on you to answer a question? You felt excitement if you were sure of the answer and dread if you had no clue. Knowing the right answer in class always made the difference between success and failure, pride and embarrassment.

1. How confident do you feel that you can give a correct answer when you are asked a question about the Bible? Mark the continuum.

Very confident   Very afraid

Psalm 19:7 teaches that God's Word can make the "inexperienced wise." Whether you are a novice at Bible study or a long-time reader of Scripture, it can revive you and give you wisdom for daily living.

Psalm 19:7

"The instruction of the LORD is perfect, reviving the soul; the testimony of the LORD is trustworthy, making the inexperienced wise."

2. Name an area of your life in which you currently need God's wisdom.
   School, home

We must be able to understand the Bible's teachings to benefit from its wisdom. When Israel was returning from exile in Babylon, God chose Nehemiah to lead the nation to rebuild Jerusalem. In the midst of their physical labor, the people asked the priests to publicly bring out the law of Moses and read it to them. During the long reading the **Levites*** moved through the crowd, "giving the meaning so that the people could understand what was read" (Nehemiah 8:8).

Levites: descendants of the Israelite tribe of Levi, who acted as assistants to the priests in the temple

It's OK to admit that God's Word is sometimes difficult to understand. After all, it is the immortal God's self-revelation to mortals with finite minds. In Israel's history God gave the tribe of Levi the responsibility of temple duty, including the study and explanation of His law. To believers under the new covenant of Christ's salvation, God has granted His Holy Spirit so that we no longer need a priest to understand His Word.

3. Read John 14:26 in the margin. How does the Holy Spirit help believers who seek God's truth?

will teach you all things and remind you of everything I have told you.

John 14:26

"The Counselor, the Holy Spirit—the Father will send Him in My name—will teach you all things and remind you of everything I have told you."

As we study God's Word, the Holy Spirit teaches us God's truth. After we have studied, He helps us recall what we have learned. Knowing that the Spirit will help us understand God's Word, we can be confident in approaching it for study and application to our lives.

We can begin to understand the Word by asking the proper questions. Here are five we can use as a starting point.

1. *How does this verse or passage reveal God's character?* The whole Bible is primarily about God. When you approach Scripture, don't simply look for moral instruction or personal direction. Always begin by allowing God to speak about Himself.

2. *How does the passage reveal God's redemptive* plan?* God reveals Himself to us so that we can be reconciled to Him. After you identify what you can learn about Him, seek to know how you can properly relate to Him.

3. *What objections do I raise against the truth found in the passage?* Pride is always ready to rear its ugly head. Identifying ways you resist God's truth prepares you to apply it to your life.

4. *How did the passage apply to the original hearers?* The Bible cannot mean now what it never meant then. Understanding the original context of a passage will help you interpret it correctly.

5. *How does this truth address my relationship with Christ?* Scripture is full of eternal truth, but it is also God's personal communication to each person. Always seek to understand how you need to personally apply a passage to your relationship with your King.

Redemption: the act of recovering what was lost. God's redemptive activity was accomplished by the sacrifice of Christ.

4. Turn to page 99 and use "Scripture-Passage Worksheet" to study John 15:1-8.

5. Before going further in this study, take time to read "Bible-Study Tools" on pages 100–101 and "Recommended Resources" on page 102. This information will help you gather resources that will aid your study of God's Word.

Day 2 • Reading for All Its Worth

God's Word for Today
"Your words were found, and I ate them. Your words became a delight to me and the joy of my heart, for I am called by Your name, LORD God of Hosts." Jeremiah 15:16

↕ Read and meditate on "God's Word for Today" in the margin. Spend a moment in prayer as you begin today's lesson.

① What is your favorite book? _John / Ephisians_

Some people love to read, while others feel it a terrible chore. Unfortunately, I have found that whenever I start to read the Bible, a million temptations seek to dissuade me. The prophet Jeremiah saw God's words as an opportunity to feast. When God spoke, it was a delight and a joy for Jeremiah. It should be for us as well.

What is the greatest distraction or obstacle that tends to keep you from reading the Bible?
Phone / T.V

Today we will look at some ways you can feast on God's Word.

Read the Bible as panorama. We typically read the Bible in an unusual way. Often we start at the midpoint of it entirely, in the middle of a book, and sometimes in the middle of an account. Our reasons are admirable: we want to understand a particular truth for a specific circumstance. But we also need to see the broad themes and messages of the Bible as a whole.

② **Have you read the Bible completely through?** ○ Yes ◉ No
If not, what has kept you from doing so? Check all that apply.
◉ Time   ○ Don't like to read
○ Fear of not understanding   ○ Not a priority
◉ Distractions (describe): _Phone School Chores_

The Bible is the sweeping epic of God's glory, magnified in humanity as He pursues the redemption of creation. To read it in its entirety is to grasp the grand scope of God's plan and our part in it. To read only portions of it reduces God's Word to a reference book. Perhaps it is time to stop treating the Bible as if it were a recipe book for successful living and begin seeing it as the heroic account it truly is.

The Bible I am reading from today is 1,252 pages in length. To read it in a month would mean reading 40 or 41 pages a day. To read it in three months would mean reading 13 or 14 pages a day. To read it in one year would mean reading only 3 or 4 pages a day. Can we not give that much time to God?

Read the Bible in parts. Though it is important to read the Bible in its entirety to get the big picture, you still need to read it in parts to observe the details. As you read the Bible for the panoramic view, you will certainly want to pause time after time to dig into a particular narrative, teaching, chapter, or verse. When you come to a passage that piques your interest and addresses your current life situation, take time to read it again and again. Repeatedly reading particular parts of the Bible will enable you to fully understand their impact on your life.

Just as understanding the whole of Scripture will help you understand particular passages, the reverse is true as well. Developing a detailed knowledge of the Bible will help you know how God has woven the agenda for His kingdom through each part of history.

③ What is your favorite account in the Bible? _parable of the lost son_
Why? _it relatable and true_

Listen to the Bible read aloud. When people in Nehemiah's day called for God's Word to be read to them, they stood for approximately six hours to listen to it (see Nehemiah 8:3). Today movies over two hours, business meetings lasting longer than an hour, or sermons of more than 30 minutes are often considered too long. Yet the Hebrew people had such a longing to hear from God that they stood in rapt attention for half the day to listen.

Reading the Bible aloud or listening to an audio recording presents another avenue to discover the epic drama of God's story and to internalize its message. Hearing God's Word read can bring the action and truth to life in a fresh way.

④ Examine "Bible-Reading Plans" on page 103. Make a commitment today that you will begin reading the Bible in its entirety. Identify any other changes you would like to make in the way you read the Bible.

_____

> Repeatedly reading particular parts of the Bible will enable you to fully understand their impact on your life.

Nehemiah 8:3
"While [Ezra] was facing the square in front of the Water Gate, he read out of it from daybreak until noon before the men, the women, and those who could understand. All the people listened attentively to the book of the law."

Day 3 • Meditating and Memorizing

 Read and meditate on "God's Word for Today" in the margin. Spend a moment in prayer as you begin today's lesson.

I have heard it said that reading the Bible without meditating on it is like trying to eat without swallowing. It is one thing to get a taste of your favorite food and another to physically benefit from it. When all we do is glance at the greatness of God's Word, we do not allow its Author to change us. Meditation allows the power of the Word to repeatedly wash over our lives.

Meditation seems foreign to our modern understanding of Christianity. The concept is commonly associated with Chinese monks chanting mantras and New Age followers attempting to become one with nature. Yet we see the word used numerous times in the Bible.

1. What purpose of meditation is identified in "God's Word for Today"?

 _____

It is important that we deliberately reflect on Scripture to avoid sin and for a number of other reasons identified in Psalm 119. While pagan meditation seeks to detach oneself from authority, Christian meditation leads us to submit our will to God's Word.

Of the 11 times *meditate* is found in the Bible (HCSB), 10 are in Psalms, where the writer contemplates God's work and words. We also find the concept in other places in Scripture. Joshua 1:8 says to meditate on or "recite" God's instruction day and night. Meditating on God's Word forces us to leave behind the busyness of our lives for the greater business of learning God's Word.

Meditation benefits our lives in several ways.
1. Meditation stops our minds from churning on problems, temptations, and our own solutions so that we hear from God.
2. Meditation elevates God's Word to its rightful places as the standard for our lives. We spiritually evaluate our lives against the truth of God's Word instead of comparing our "goodness" to the life of a neighbor.

3. Meditation gives us time to apply God's Word to our circumstances. Too often we study the Bible to appease our guilty consciences or to increase our knowledge. Meditation increases the likelihood that we will apply God's truth to our lives.

② How would meditation help you with a particular issue in your life?

Help you concentrate?

Another method of repeated exposure to God's Word is memorization. I can already hear your objections: my memory is bad; I haven't memorized anything since I was in school; I've got too many other things to remember. Do you see the one constant factor in all of the objections—"I"? Don't overlook God's power to help you memorize Scripture. If you continually place God, His kingdom, and His will at the center of your life, you will find that you can memorize His Word of truth.

③ How do you think Scripture memorization would strengthen your daily walk with God?

You know more about him

> If you continually place God, His kingdom, and His will at the center of your life, you will find that you can memorize His Word of truth.

Here are a few practical suggestions for memorizing Scripture:
1. Use memory cards like those provided at the back of this book.
2. Repeat the verse(s) aloud three times a day for 30 days.
3. Apply the verse to a current situation in your life.

④ Use "Tips for Memorizing Scripture" on page 104 to discover other practical ideas for committing Scripture to memory.

Pray and agree with God's Word that meditation and memorization would draw you closer to Him by keeping His truth in your heart and mind. Ask Him to help you make these practices a priority and to help you apply His Word to your life. Write this week's memory verse and pray it as a commitment to God.

Help me understand your instruction and I will obey it and follow it with all my heart

Day 4 • Understanding Genres

God's Word for Today

"Ezra had determined in his heart to study the law of the LORD, obey it, and teach its statutes and ordinances in Israel." Ezra 7:10

 Genre: a type or category of writing having a particular form, content, or technique. Examples are history, poetry, prophecy, and letters.

↕ Read and meditate on "God's Word for Today" in the margin.
Spend a moment in prayer as you begin today's lesson.

In "God's Word for Today" we find Ezra leaving Babylon and arriving in Jerusalem. Ezra was "skilled in the law" (Ezra 7:6) given by God. In fact, the Babylonian king Artaxerxes recognized God's favor on Ezra and aided him in his journey back to Jerusalem, where God used him as an instrument for a great spiritual awakening (see Nehemiah 8–10). We should hope to emulate Ezra's determination to understand God's Word.

The Bible contains several different **genres*** of writing. Understanding the characteristics of each biblical genre will help us discern the message God wanted to convey to us. The primary types of literature used in the Bible are history, poetry, prophecy, and letters.

① **Without doing research, match each Bible book with its genre.**

   a 1. Nehemiah   a. History
   b 2. Ecclesiastes   b. Poetry
   b 3. Psalms   c. Prophecy
   c 4. Jeremiah   d. Letter
   a 5. Matthew
   d 6. Colossians
   c 7. Revelation

History. Some biblical literature is historical and is therefore intended to be interpreted literally. Studying historical narratives such as Exodus or the Gospel of Luke requires that we treat them as fact. God inspired the writers of the historical books to record the occurrences of events such as the history of Israel throughout the Old Testament, the life of Christ in the Gospels, and the beginning of the church in Acts. As you study the historical books, realize that you are reading an explanation of what happened to a particular group of people at a particular time and in particular circumstances. We can learn the principles of how God worked then and apply the lessons to our day. However, we must not expect that God will always repeat the same actions throughout all of history.

Answers to activity 1: 1-a, 2-b, 3-b, 4-c, 5-a, 6-d, 7-c

Poetry. As we study poetic books and portions of Scripture, we must remain aware that they use **symbols*** and other **figures of speech***. The Books of Job, Psalms, Proverbs, Ecclesiastes, and Song of Songs are all poetic. Job, a very ancient poem, records the trials of a godly man. Psalms, a collection of songs used by the Hebrews in worship, uses many literary devices to describe the power of God and the plight of humanity. Proverbs and Ecclesiastes are collections of teachings about the search for wisdom in the kingdom of God. The Song of Songs is a metaphorical poem about romantic love and the beginning of marriage.

2) Read Psalm 104:2 and Proverbs 4:6 in the margin and underline the figures of speech used.

Prophecy. The prophetic books of the Bible are generally classified as Major Prophets, Minor Prophets, and New Testament prophecy. The delineation between major and minor prophecies in the Old Testament is determined only by the length of the book, not by the topics covered. The New Testament also includes a prophetic book. Revelation is an apocalyptic prophecy describing the fulfillment of God's redemption in human history.

In studying prophecy, we must take care to understand the symbolism used. Remember that the writers were describing God-inspired revelations that had not been witnessed in real life. The prophetic books are difficult to understand; but by first recognizing the original context of the book, we can begin to properly grasp the message.

3) Read Ezekiel 37:1-14 and name the primary symbol used. _____
How did this symbol serve to dramatize the message God wanted to convey to Israel?

IDK

_____

Letters. Most of the New Testament books fall into the categories of Pauline or General **Epistles***. The letters from Paul, Peter, and others to the early congregations taught doctrine and how to live as citizens of God's kingdom. Because most of these letters are highly structured, they are easily outlined for understanding.

4) Review "Outline of the Bible" on page 94. Which genre of biblical literature do you feel that you best learn from? Why?

✳ *Symbol:* a concrete word used to represent an abstract idea or concept

✳ *Figure of speech:* a form of expression that conveys meaning by comparing an unfamiliar concept with a familiar one

Psalm 104:2
"[God] wraps Himself in light as if it were a robe, spreading out the sky like a canopy."

Proverbs 4:6
"Don't abandon wisdom, and she will watch over you; love her, and she will guard you."

✳ *Epistle:* a letter inspired by God, written by an early church leader, and subsequently included in God's Word

Day 5 • Two Major Themes

Read and mediate on "God's Word for Today" in the margin.
Spend a moment in prayer as you begin today's lesson.

God's Word for Today

"Be diligent to present yourself approved to God, a worker who doesn't need to be ashamed, correctly teaching the word of truth."
2 Timothy 2:15

As Paul wrote to the young pastor Timothy, he encouraged him to engage in "correctly teaching the word of truth" (2 Timothy 2:15). The compound word he used in the Greek language for "correctly teaching" literally means *to cut straight.* It is a term used in carpentry and construction for properly cutting lumber or stones so that items would be well built. We must apply similar diligence to the study and teaching of God's Word.

When we pick up a book and read it, we eventually ask, "What is the major point the author is trying to make?" Apply that question to the Bible.

 What do you think are two major themes of God's Word?

<u>Teaching + loving</u>
<u>Gods Covenant, Gods Kingdom</u>

A multitude of lessons are taught in the Bible, so choosing only a couple is difficult. However, understanding two general themes can give us a broad overview of God's Word—God's covenant and God's kingdom.

God's covenant. From the beginning of creation, God sought a covenant relationship with humankind. From Adam and Eve's simple dependency on God's provision to the complex law given to Israel, God made a path for people to relate to Him. The study of God's Word leads to this great understanding: God has told us about Himself so that we can enter a relationship with Him.

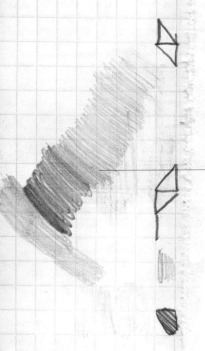

Covenant: a contract or agreement expressing God's gracious promises to His people and their relationship with Him

The only true way for us to know God is by way of a **covenant.*** In a covenant two parties make oaths of allegiance to each other. Each party must commit to be faithful to the other; otherwise, the covenant is useless. The word *covenant* is used hundreds of times throughout the Bible to depict God's relationship with humanity, as well as relationships between people.

 Identify the person with whom God made a covenant in each passage.
Genesis 6: <u>Mark</u>   Genesis 15: <u>Luke</u>

God first established a covenant with Noah by saving his family from the great flood in Genesis 6. In Genesis 15 God established a covenant with Abraham to create the nation of Israel, His people.

At the Last Supper Christ announced the new covenant He was beginning with people who would submit to His lordship.

 Read Matthew 26:28 in the margin. What sealed the covenant between God and people who wanted forgiveness for their sins?

His Blood

As Jesus prepared for His death and resurrection, He informed the apostles of the new covenant God was establishing through the perfect sacrifice for sin. That covenant was sealed with the body and blood of Jesus. A covenant with God is lopsided. He does all the work, and we gain all the benefits. The new covenant established by the sacrifice of Jesus allows us to be reconciled with God forever.

God's kingdom. A second general theme that runs throughout the Bible is God's kingdom. Ultimately, everything is under God's control. The Bible teaches us about His rule and His kingdom. Jesus taught about the kingdom of God and invited people to enter it. The Gospel of Mark uses the phrase "kingdom of God" 14 times, and it is the first subject Jesus spoke about in the book.

 Read Mark 1:15 in the margin. In the final phrase how did Jesus describe the arrival of God's kingdom?

Belive in the good news

The coming of the kingdom is good news! In the Model Prayer Jesus instructed His disciples to pray for the coming of God's kingdom (see Matthew 6:9-13). We should eagerly study God's Word with a view toward participating in His kingdom work.

 Spend time in prayer thanking God for His covenant with you through His Son and for including you in His kingdom. Ask Him to teach you about these themes as you study His Word.

 Write this week's Scripture-memory verse in the margin.

Matthew 26:28
"This is My blood that establishes the covenant; it is shed for many for the forgiveness of sins."

Mark 1:15
"The time is fulfilled, and the kingdom of God has come near. Repent and believe in the good news!"

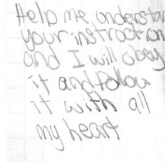

Help me understand your instruction and I will obey it and follow it with all my heart

Week 4 » Day 5

63

Session 4 • How to Study the Word

WELCOME AND PRAYER
Welcome participants and pray for God's guidance during the discussion.

OPENING ACTIVITY
1. Invite a participant to recite this week's memory verse.
2. Describe your first experience studying the Bible on your own. Was it easy or frustrating?
3. Name the primary distractions and temptations that discourage us from studying God's Word.

REVIEW OF DAILY WORK
1. Review the five questions in day 1 that we should ask when studying a Scripture passage. Use the questions to examine Philippians 2:5-11.
   • How does this verse or passage reveal God's character?
   • How does the passage reveal God's redemptive plan?
   • What objections do you raise against the truth found in the passage?
   • How did the passage apply to the original hearers?
   • How does this truth address your relationship with Christ?

2. Define *genre* (p. 60). Learning the different genres represented in Scripture can help us understand and apply God's Word. Identify the genres used by biblical writers. Which genre of Scripture do you most enjoy reading? Why?

GROUP DISCUSSION

Discover
1. What are two major themes of Scripture, as identified in day 5?
2. Define *covenant* (p. 62). How do you understand your relationship with God as a covenant?
3. How do you see the theme of God's kingdom at work in the mission of the church?

Connect
Your memory verse for the week is Psalm 119:34. Describe the type of devotion it calls us to have toward God's Word. How will this deep devotion affect the way we treat coworkers? Relate to God? Face temptation?

Relate

1. Meditation sometimes seems to be a concept hijacked by other religions and cults. Define *meditation* from a biblical perspective (day 3).
2. Read Joshua 1:8. Discuss how we can maintain our focus on God's Word in the midst of daily activities.
3. Have you ever taken time to meditate on a passage of Scripture? Describe your experience. What types of lessons did you learn?

Confront

How will memorizing Scripture change the way you function at your place of employment? Relate to your family? Maintain obedience to God's mission in the world?

Change

1. Are you ready to make a commitment to read the entire Bible? Refer to Bible-Reading Plans" on page 103 and discuss which idea would be best for you.
2. Read Psalm 119:11. Name some practical ways to memorize Scripture. Review "Tips for Memorizing Scripture" on page 104.

MISSIONAL APPLICATION

What is the benefit of reading the Bible as panoramic story? Of studying particular passages closely? Of hearing or reading Scripture aloud? (See day 2.)

PREVIEW WEEK 5

Turn to page 67 and preview the study for the coming week.

PRAYING TOGETHER

Close the session in prayer for one another.

Week 5

Living the Word

"Be doers of the word
and not hearers only,
deceiving yourselves."
James 1:22

Living the Word

Our lives seem to be an ocean of noise with an occasional island of quiet. We are so overrun with information, knowledge, and insight that we rarely have time to process any of it and actually put it into practice. We know how to exercise, but who has time? We understand how we should eat, but fast food is easier. We see that our kids need more time with us, but work drains our energy. Knowing what to do and actually doing it often seem very distant from each other.

God doesn't reveal His character, will, and kingdom to us through His Word so that we will know more. Rather, God is calling us through His Word to live differently. By the grace we receive through faith in Christ, we can live in step with God's glory and can see His image come to light within us.

This week I hope you will slow down enough to begin practicing what you are learning from the Word. We have learned that God's Word has the power to change our lives, but we must take the steps that allow it to do so.

OVERVIEW OF WEEK 5
Day 1: Listening, Then Doing
Day 2: Love That Shows
Day 3: Deep Devotion
Day 4: Praying the Word
Day 5: Solid Decision Making

VERSE TO MEMORIZE
"Be doers of the word and not hearers only, deceiving yourselves" (James 1:22).

DISCIPLESHIP HELPS FOR WEEK 4
"Prayers of the Bible" (p. 105)
"Prayer Exercise" (p. 106)

Day 1 • Listening, Then Doing

God's Word for Today

"Be doers of the word and not hearers only, deceiving yourselves." James 1:22

Read and meditate on "God's Word for Today" (this week's verse to memorize) in the margin. Spend a moment in prayer as you begin today's lesson. Remove the Scripture-memory card for week 5 from the back of your book and begin committing this verse to memory.

I told you earlier that I'm a book junkie. I'm also a news-and-information junkie. Knowing new things and processing information get all of my brain synapses firing. But simply knowing new information does me no good unless it changes the way I live.

Solomon, the third king of Israel, had a similar problem. God granted him so much wisdom that he surpassed everyone else in history (see 1 Kings 3:12). Yet even with all that understanding, Solomon chased power, wealth, and pleasure trying to find happiness. His cynical journey is recorded in the Book of Ecclesiastes. But chapter 5 records an unusual respite from Solomon's frantic search for meaning.

Ecclesiastes 5:1-3

"Guard your step when you go to the house of God. Better to draw near in obedience than to offer the sacrifice as fools do, for they are ignorant and do wrong. Do not be hasty to speak, and do not be impulsive to make a speech before God. God is in heaven and you are on earth, so let your words be few. For dreams result from much work and a fool's voice from many words."

1. Read Ecclesiastes 5:1-3 in the margin. Check the things Solomon emphasized.
   ○ Obedience   ○ Speaking to God   ○ Sacrifice   ○ Silence

In the middle of the book, Solomon stopped long enough to realize that silence before God is necessary: it is "better to draw near in obedience than to offer that sacrifice as fools do" (v. 2). Solomon had a great deal of knowledge, but it did not always translate into obedience to God's laws. He needed to walk quietly before God so as to hear and obey. He had likely heard priests read and teach all of God's law. But was he obeying it?

2. Has your knowledge of God's Word outpaced your obedience to it?
   ○ Yes   ○ No

God's Word is His message to be heeded. It is not for entertainment, casual enlightenment, or good advice. Solomon reminded us who is on earth and who is in heaven. When we see the Bible in light of our position to its Author, obedience begins to make a great deal of sense. God has given His revelation so that we can live it in order to become like Christ.

The New Testament Book of James was written to the early believers to encourage their maturity in the faith. "God's Word for Today" defines what maturity looks like: "Be doers of the word" (James 1:22). Like Solomon, the believers had most likely heard God's Word and were intimately acquainted with the gospel. But James reminded them of the key element for growing in their faith: obedience to what they had already learned.

③ **Listed below are some lessons you have probably learned from God's Word. Circle the ones you are actively obeying. Place an *X* beside the ones you need to begin obeying.**
- ○ Worship in spirit and truth.
- ○ Pray daily.
- ○ Care for the helpless.
- ○ Tell others about Jesus.
- ○ Love others, even your enemies (see Matthew 5:43-48).
- ○ Show unity with the church.

④ **When God gave the Old Testament law to the people of Israel, He did so with a certain result in mind. Read Deuteronomy 29:29 in the margin and underline the reason God gave His Word to His people.**

Deuteronomy 29:29
"The hidden things belong to the LORD our God, but the revealed things belong to us and our children forever, so that we may follow all the words of this law."

In Scripture God tells us not only about Himself but also how we are to live. If we learned only about God's nature, we would be in miserable fear because we could never please Him. If all He told us was how to behave, we would be unhappy workers, not knowing why we have to act a certain way. Instead, we have the gift of knowing both God's nature and His laws.

When we think about obeying God's Word, there is no better place to start than with the Great Commission. Before Jesus ascended to heaven, He commanded us to "make disciples of all nations" (Matthew 28:19). We recognize our duty to spread the message of Christ, we celebrate when others do it, and we see opportunities to personally share the gospel. But do we obey by actually sharing the good news? Let's make a commitment to be not just hearers of the Word but doers as well.

In Scripture God tells us not only about Himself but also how we are to live.

⑤ **Name three persons with whom you would like to share Christ.**

1. _____

2. _____

3. _____

Day 2 • Love That Shows

God's Word for Today

"The one who has My commandments and keeps them is the one who loves Me. And the one who loves Me will be loved by My Father. I also will love him and will reveal Myself to him." John 14:21

Read and meditate on "God's Word for Today" in the margin. Spend a moment in prayer as you begin today's lesson.

1. **How do you express love to your family? Check all that apply.**
   ○ Verbal affirmations   ○ Hugs   ○ Rewards/gifts
   ○ Joking around   ○ Time with one another
   ○ Other: _____

Love is an odd thing. It is both a choice and an emotion. Love means caring and sacrifice. Love happens between spouses, children, and friends. But we also love things like our dogs, houses, and hamburgers. Scripture teaches us how love is expressed.

In John 15 Jesus was teaching the apostles about intimacy with God. He used the metaphor of vine, representing God, and branches, representing us, to show our total dependence on the Father. Then Jesus described His own love for us as being equal to the love the Father had shown Him. Due to their perfect relationship, Jesus had kept every commandment given by the Father. Jesus then called His followers to the same standard, offering them the same reward.

John 15:9-11

"As the Father has loved Me, I have also loved you. Remain in My love. If you keep My commands you will remain in My love, just as I have kept My Father's commands and remain in His love. I have spoken these things to you so that My joy may be in you and your joy may be complete."

2. **Read John 15:9-11. What is the reward for keeping Jesus' commands?**
   _____

Jesus didn't give us any room to wiggle away from this teaching. We are to show our love for Him by obeying His commands. If we keep His commands, we remain in His love.

In "God's Word for Today," John 14:21, Jesus made the same point. Obedience to God's commands and love are partners, not adversaries, in our relationship with the Lord.

3. **Define *love* and *obedience* in your own words.**
   Love: _____
   _____
   Obedience: _____

Creating definitions of *love* and *obedience* may have taken a few minutes, but what if I asked you to define *loving obedience* or *obedient love?* We usually don't pair the two words. Why? Because we are rebellious by nature and don't like to obey. But in a relationship with Christ, love serves as the motivation for obedience, and obedience serves as the expression of our love for Him. Love is the heart, and obedience is the hand. Love is the energy, and obedience is the tool. One without the other is useless.

④ **Check the statement that is true of you.**
   ○ My pattern of obedience to God's Word indicates great love for God.
   ○ My pattern of obedience to God's Word reveals a rebellious heart.

Jesus said when we obey God's Word, His joy will take up residence in our lives (see John 15:11). That promise alone should motivate us to study and obey God's Word.

⑤ **Check the statement that is true of you.**
   ○ Joy is lacking in my life.
   ○ My study of God's Word brings me great joy.

If you want to be more obedient to God's Word, the Great Commandment is a good place to start. When a **scribe*** asked Jesus what the greatest commandment was, He said loving God and loving our neighbors (see Mark 12:29-31). Jesus also included the Shema in His answer: "Hear, O Israel! The Lord our God is one Lord." The Shema is the oldest of all theological declarations by the Hebrew people. In a time when the culture believed in a multitude of gods, Israel stood alone in declaring the existence of the one true God. Without this belief as the standard, the rest of Jesus' command does not hold any weight. If multiple deities existed whom we had to satisfy, we would be lost. But because we know God is God and has no rivals, completely loving Him makes sense. And if He requires us to love our neighbor in a way that is equal to our own self-preserving love, then we must do so. We will find joy in obedience to His Word.

⑥ **Give an example of how you can love God in each area Jesus named.**
   Heart: _____
   Soul: _____
   Mind: _____
   Strength: _____

In a relationship with Christ, love serves as the motivation for obedience, and obedience serves as the expression of our love for Him.

**Scribe:* an expert in interpreting the Old Testament law

Mark 12:29-31
" 'This is the most important,' Jesus answered: 'Listen Israel! The Lord our God, the Lord is One. Love the Lord your God will all your heart, with all your soul, with all your mind, and with all your strength. The second is: Love your neighbor as yourself. There is no other commandment greater than these.' "

Day 3 • Deep Devotion

God's Word for Today

"Let the message about the Messiah dwell richly among you, teaching and admonishing one another in all wisdom, and singing psalms, hymns, and spiritual songs, with gratitude in your hearts to God." Colossians 3:16

Read and meditate on "God's Word for Today" in the margin.
Spend a moment in prayer as you begin today's lesson.

Growing up in Birmingham, Alabama, I learned early in life that one event was more important than all others during the year—the Iron Bowl. For the uninitiated to college football, this is the annual rivalry between the University of Alabama and Auburn University. It is a game that men, women, and children discuss 365 days a year. It causes fractures in friendships and families. The word *obsessive* does not even begin to describe the level of devotion some people show to their team during the football season.

1) **List things to which people in your community show deep devotion.**

_____

"God's Word for Today," Colossians 3:16, teaches that Christians are to show deep devotion to God's Word. We are to let the "message about the Messiah dwell richly" in our lives. Writing to the church in Colosse, Paul included this admonition in the context of teaching about love (v. 14), peace (v. 15), and giving thanks (v. 17). Devotion to God's Word is a central element in living the Christian life.

2) **Showing deep devotion to God's Word takes time and effort. Check the practices you want to begin because of your devotion to Scripture.**
   ○ Memorize Scripture
   ○ Read the entire Bible
   ○ Study more closely
   ○ Use God's Word as my weapon when tempted to sin
   ○ Correct my behavior
   ○ Other: _____

If we turn to the Old Testament Book of Ecclesiastes again, we make an interesting discovery.

Ecclesiastes 12:13-14

"When all has been heard, the conclusion of the matter is: fear God and keep His commands, because this is for all humanity. For God will bring every act to judgment, including every hidden thing, whether good or evil."

3) **Read Ecclesiastes 12:13-14 in the margin. What was Solomon's conclusion after his lifelong search for meaning in life?**

_____

Solomon had shown a deep devotion to selfish pleasure of all sorts, such as power, riches, and lust. By the end of his search, he discovered that being in awe of God and obeying His Word were the only things worthy of his devotion. The same is true for us. At the end of our days, God will examine our lives to judge their worth. By the power of our Messiah's message, we have the hope of His salvation. Without it we are doomed. Devotion to God's Word produces a life that honors God and serves His kingdom.

Devotion to God's Word also has a plural dimension. Solomon's call to keep God's commands is for "all humanity" (Ecclesiastes 12:13). In Colossians 3:16 the phrase "among you" is plural. Paul's entire passage deals with the lives of Christians together in their relationship with God. Personal devotion to God's Word is lived publicly.

Paul's letter to the Galatian church presents a way we can live our devotion to God's Word.

(4) **Read Galatians 6:1-2 in the margin. How can we fulfill the law of Christ, that is, obey His commands?**

_____

After extensive teaching about freedom in Christ, Paul called on believers to carry one another's burdens. We learn how to "fulfill the law of Christ" when we live our devotion to Scripture among other people.

In 2005 I planted a church in a community that is probably much like yours—lots of casual friendships but very few deep relationships. Our devotion to God's Word should change the way we interact with one another. Your faith is personal, but God never intended for it to be private. People around you are hurting because of their sin and life circumstances. Allow your devotion to God's Word to change forever the way you interact with the people around you.

 Write down the names of friends—saved and unsaved—whose burdens you can help bear. Pray and ask God to show you how He wants you to help and how you can minister through His Word.

_____

(5) **Write this week's Scripture-memory verse in the margin.**

Personal devotion to God's Word is lived publicly.

Galatians 6:1-2
"Brothers, if someone is caught in any wrongdoing, you who are spiritual should restore such a person with a gentle spirit, watching out for yourselves so you won't be tempted also. Carry one another's burdens; in this way you will fulfill the law of Christ."

Day 4 • Praying the Word

Read and meditate on "God's Word for Today" in the margin.
Spend a moment in prayer as you begin today's lesson.

God's Word for Today

"Pray constantly."
1 Thessalonians 5:17

Having grown up in church, I have heard thousands of prayers prayed in public. And as a pastor, I continued a tradition known in many churches—asking a church member to pray before the offering was received. In these prayers I've heard and prayed the phrase "Lord, bless the gift and the giver" far too many times.

1 Write some phrases you frequently use in prayer or hear others use.

_____

We will never be able to pray perfectly until God brings His redemptive work in us to completion, but we can learn to pray better and more often. Most people agree that we should pray more, but the Bible tells us to "pray constantly" (1 Thessalonians 5:17). I frequently run out of material for lunch conversations. How am I supposed to talk to God all day long?

2 How do you think a believer can pray constantly? _____

_____

_____

Prayer is not an interruption of our outward life and thoughts but a partner to them all.

Constant prayer seems impossible, but J. I. Packer described it this way: "The whole of a Christian's thought life should be bathed, or perhaps we should say housed, in prayer."[1] Prayer is not an interruption of our outward life and thoughts but a partner to them all.

3 What do you usually pray about? Check all that apply.
○ Daily material needs   ○ Spiritual guidance
○ Decisions   ○ Worship, praise, thanksgiving
○ Healing   ○ Others' problems and needs
○ Other: _____

What areas of your life do you need to include in your prayers?

_____

_____

One of the most effective ways to pray is through the ancient practice of praying Scripture. Praying God's Word ensures that we speak clearly, ask rightly, and meditate properly. Packer put it this way: "With the Bible as our prayer book, we will never be short of broodings and beacons to shape our praying."[2]

④ **Read "Prayers of the Bible" on page 105. Circle three of the prayers you would like to use in your prayer life.**

Scripture meditation, memorization, and constant prayer all allow you to pray God's Word to Him. By placing your prayer life under the authority of Scripture, you will be assured of praying thoughts and words that honor God and that help align your heart with His will.

Here are some examples of ways to use God's Word in your prayer life.

Use Matthew 6:9-13 as a model. Commonly referred to as the Lord's Prayer, this passage is better understood as Jesus' Model Prayer for us. The parallel passage in Luke 11 shows that Jesus provided this model in response to the disciples' request "Lord, teach us to pray" (Luke 11:1). The Model Prayer gives us insight into the basic components of prayer.

Use Psalm 51 to confess sin. With sorrow and passion David confessed his sin and sought God's forgiveness. We are often short of words to say when we feel guilty. Psalm 51 is a beautiful place to rest when we don't know how to ask for God's forgiveness.

Use Jude 24-25 to celebrate God's greatness. We experience joyful frustration when we seek to praise God, because fully describing Him is impossible. Jude's doxology helps you praise God when you run short of words.

Use Ephesians 3:14-21 for spiritual maturity. Maybe you want to mature in your faith but do not know what to do next. Paul's prayer for the Ephesian church provides a great outline of how to pray for maturity.

⑤ **Turn to "Prayer Exercise" on page 106 and follow the directions to use Psalm 23 in prayer today. Write your impressions of this experience.**

_____

_____

> Praying God's Word ensures that we speak clearly, ask rightly, and meditate properly.

1. J. I. Packer and Carolyn Nystrom, *Praying* (Downers Grove: Inter-Varsity Press, 2006), 75.
2. Ibid., 94.

Week 5 » Day 4

God's Word for Today

"Everyone who hears these words of Mine and acts on them will be like a sensible man who built his house on the rock." Matthew 7:24

Matthew 7:24-27

"Everyone who hears these words of Mine and acts on them will be like a sensible man who built his house on the rock. The rain fell, the rivers rose, and the winds blew and pounded that house. Yet it didn't collapse, because its foundation was on the rock. But everyone who hears these words of Mine and doesn't act on them will be like a foolish man who built his house on the sand. The rain fell, the rivers rose, the winds blew and pounded that house, and it collapsed. And its collapse was great!"

Day 5 • Solid Decision Making

Read and meditate on "God's Word for Today" in the margin. Spend a moment in prayer as you begin today's lesson.

I truly enjoy a great story. Over the past few years I have found myself returning to the classics for leisure reading. Authors like H. G. Wells, Robert Louis Stevenson, and Sir Arthur Conan Doyle tell great stories that draw me into them. When I read their stories, I find myself involved, learning something new about life and how to live it well.

Jesus eclipses even the greatest writers as the master storyteller. He told His stories in the form of parables. As Jesus concluded the longest of His sermons recorded in the Bible, he told a parable of two men and their attempts at home construction.

 Read Jesus' parable in the margin and answer the following questions.

What two foundations were chosen? _____

What common trial did the men face? _____

What were the two different results of the storm? _____

_____

Jesus presented this story as the conclusion to His sermon on fully living the principles of His kingdom. The two men in the story had the same objective: to build a home. The homes being built represent lives to be lived.

The two men had to make a crucial choice about the foundations for their homes. Until a foundation is chosen, nothing else can be constructed. The same is true of living life: we adopt a worldview or life philosophy; then we make decisions based on that foundation. The first man chose a foundation of rock, while the second man chose sand.

Notice that Jesus' emphasis was on doing. The difference between the two men was that one—the "sensible man" (v. 24)—not only heard Jesus' words but also acted on them. The one who didn't act on Jesus' words is described as foolish (see v. 26). Both men heard Jesus' words, but only one chose to build his life on them. Living the Word takes more than merely hearing it. We must live by it.

2 This week's memory verse, James 1:22, stresses living the Word. Write the verse here.

_____

_____

In Jesus' parable both men encountered a fierce storm, but the outcome was different for each man. Built on the rock, the reasonable man's home withstood the wind and rain. However, the foolish man's home succumbed to the storm and collapsed. Weathering the storm depended on choosing the right foundation.

3 When you face a difficult choice, how do you make a decision? Check all that apply.

○ Ask family/friends for advice   ○ Decide without help
○ Observe others' decisions   ○ Pray
○ Ask someone to decide for you   ○ Procrastinate
○ Flip a coin   ○ Consult the Bible
○ Other: _____

Every day we make critical decisions. These decisions affect not only us personally but also our marriages, children, coworkers, neighbors, family, and friends. But too often our decision making is based on our own wit and best guesses. In contrast, Jesus offers us His Word as the foundation for solid decision making.

Read Proverbs 3:5-6 in the margin. Living in God's Word assures you of having God's guidance in the large and small issues of life. Right now you are probably facing a decision in your life. Allow God's Word to be your guide so that your decision will reflect His wisdom and bring Him glory.

4 Think about a decision are you currently facing. How will putting God's Word into practice make a difference in the decision you make?

_____

_____

_____

Living the Word takes more than merely hearing it. We must live by it.

Proverbs 3:5-6
"Trust in the LORD with all your heart, and do not rely on your own understanding; think about Him in all your ways, and He will guide you on the right paths."

Session 5 • Living the Word

WELCOME AND PRAYER
Welcome participants and pray for God's guidance during the discussion.

OPENING ACTIVITY
1. Invite a participant to recite this week's memory verse.
2. What if someone gave you the pieces of a jigsaw puzzle to put together without showing you a picture of the completed puzzle? How difficult would it be to complete the puzzle?

REVIEW OF DAILY WORK
1. God's Word provides a picture of what our lives should look like in order to be like Christ. This week's study shows that God's Word affects every part of our lives. What is an area of your life in which you want to apply God's Word more diligently? How can you do that?
2. This week's memory verse, James 1:22, emphasizes being a doer of the Word and not just a hearer. Share responses to activity 2 on page 68. What are possible results when we are not willing to obey what we know of God's Word?

GROUP DISCUSSION

Discover
The concepts of love and obedience are not often linked. Yet Jesus did just that in John 14:21; 15:9-11. Read these passages. What is the relationship between love and obedience in the life of a follower of Christ?

Connect
1. Read Deuteronomy 29:29. God reveals His Word to us with the intention that we will follow it. Choose one of the following examples from Scripture and discuss how the person(s) did or did not follow God's Word well: King David, the 12 disciples, the apostle Paul.
2. Read Colossians 3:16. Give practical examples of how the message of Jesus' life can enrich our lives. How can our lives demonstrate devotion to God's Word?

Relate

1. Read Ecclesiastes 5:1-3. When you approach God, what gets in the way of slowing the frantic pace of life and focusing on Him?
2. How could you better experience times of stillness and silence with God's Word? How would this practice help you apply God's Word to every facet of life?

Confront

We often think decisions must be made immediately. What decision would you go back and change that you made too quickly? Share responses to activity 3 on page 77. Read Proverbs 3:5-6. How can you place God's Word at the center of your decision-making process?

Change

1. Identify decisions looming in your life and discuss how God's Word provides a foundation for decisions that will honor God.
2. Discuss ways God's Word can be used in prayer (p. 75). Share your experiences using "Prayer Exercise" on page 106.

MISSIONAL APPLICATION

The Great Commission and the Great Commandment are key Scriptures believers can immediately apply to their lives. Discuss responses to activity 5 on page 69 and activity 6 on page 71.

PREVIEW WEEK 6

Turn to page 81 and preview the study for the coming week.

PRAYING TOGETHER

Spend time in prayer for one another. Then close the session by praying one of the Scripture passages suggested on page 75.

Week 6

Spreading the Word

"What you have heard from me
in the presence of many witnesses,
commit to faithful men who will
be able to teach others also."

2 Timothy 2:2

Spreading the Word

My grandfather was the town mechanic in a small city, so my father and his two brothers grew up at the garage learning how to fix cars. When Dad entered the navy, he became a "sparky"—a systems electrician on naval aircraft. And then I came along. Some men are mechanically inclined; I am mechanically declined. I can fix only a few things, but I can break almost anything.

As a kid, I watched Dad as he worked on the family station wagon. He explained how the auto parts worked and fit together to make things whir, buzz, and hum at just the right pace. My eyes glazed over in complete ignorance. But one day the fan in my 1984 Monte Carlo broke. I didn't have the money to fix it, and Dad wasn't home to help. So at the age of 17, I dug back through my memories of Dad's lessons, looked through his repair books, and plundered his toolbox. After a few hours of bloodied knuckles and grease, the fan was fixed. The lessons from my father had not been in vain.

In our final week together it is time for you to move from learner and doer to teacher. God's Word is meant to have a lasting impact on all of human history. For that to happen, God designed us to pass along the lessons we learn to one another. This week we will look at five principles for spreading the Word.

OVERVIEW OF WEEK 6
Day 1: Leading the Next Generation
Day 2: Generous Conversations
Day 3: Calling the Wayward Home
Day 4: Caring for Outsiders
Day 5: Raising Up Leaders

VERSE TO MEMORIZE
"What you have heard from me in the presence of many witnesses, commit to faithful men who will be able to teach others also" (2 Timothy 2:2).

DISCIPLESHIP HELP FOR WEEK 6
"Seed-Scattering List" (p. 107)

Day 1 • Leading the Next Generation

↕ Read and meditate on "God's Word for Today" in the margin. Spend a moment in prayer as you begin today's lesson.

Parenting is a strange endeavor. Some days you are a stern disciplinarian, and others you are a source of fun. No matter what, your love shines through as you rear the children God has entrusted to you.

① What is the silliest thing you have done as a parent or have seen a parent do?

_____

② What is or would be your top priority in parenting?
○ A quiet house   ○ A fun home
○ Godly children   ○ Obedient children
○ Independent children   ○ Enforcing the rules
Other: _____

Parenting involves setting priorities. As a father, I set priorities for myself and help my two sons understand what theirs should be as well. The Bible has a lot to say about the relationship between parents and children. God chose the image of our Heavenly Father to help us understand who He is. Biblical passages such as Deuteronomy 6:4-9 and 11:18-25 clearly teach that God intends for one generation to pass along the teachings of His Word to the next generation.

God intends for one generation to pass along the teachings of His Word to the next generation.

③ Refer to "God's Word for Today," Deuteronomy 11:19. What are the four places where we are to teach our children about God's Word?
1. _____
2. _____
3. _____
4. _____

Parents have a responsibility to share God's Word with their children at all times and in all places. But parents are faced with a multitude of distractions to teaching God's Word to our children.

④ **Rank the top three temptations or distractions that keep parents from teaching God's Word to their children:**

___ Lack of knowledge of the Bible   ___ Busyness/career

___ Fear of hard questions   ___ Embarrassment

___ Expect the church to do it   ___ Don't know how to teach

___ Lack of good examples   ___ Lack of commitment

___ Other: _____

Circle the one that is the greatest challenge for you.

Our primary task as parents is to lead our children to follow God, not us. Though it is easier to simply have our kids live according to our rules, parents must envision lives for their children that are filled with a love for God and His Word.

⑤ **Read Proverbs 22:6 in the margin. If you are a parent, what do you hope your children's spiritual lives will look like when they are adults?**

_____

What are you currently doing to ground your kids in God's Word?

_____

Christians have often read this verse only hoping their misbehaving children will be upstanding citizens one day. God's Word envisions something more. Through God's Word our children can experience spiritual transformation. And don't stop with changing just your children's lives. God's Word is meant to be shared with all people. Psalm 145:4 in the margin says each generation must tell the next of God's "mighty acts."

Our memory verse for the week, 2 Timothy 2:2, presents a constant progression of God's Word as it reaches people who, in turn, tell it to other people. Include your children in the onward march of God's truth by instilling in them a love for and reliance on His Word.

 Ask God to help you share with your children what you are learning about His Word. Ask Him to help you make and keep this commitment.

⑥ Remove the Scripture-memory card for week 6 from the back of your book and begin committing this verse to memory.

Proverbs 22:6
"Teach a youth about the way he should go; even when he is old he will not depart from it."

Psalm 145:4
"One generation will declare Your works to the next and will proclaim Your mighty acts."

Day 2 • Generous Conversations

God's Word for Today

"This is the meaning of the parable: The seed is the word of God." Luke 8:11

Luke 8:4-8

"As a large crowd was gathering, and people were flocking to Him from every town, He said in a parable: 'A sower went out to sow his seed. As he was sowing, some fell along the path; it was trampled on, and the birds of the sky ate it up. Other seed fell on the rock; when it sprang up, it withered, since it lacked moisture. Other seed fell among thorns; the thorns sprang up with it and choked it. Still other seed fell on good ground; when it sprang up, it produced a crop: 100 times what was sown.' As He said this, He called out, 'Anyone who has ears to hear should listen!'"

Answers to activity 2:
1-d, 2-a, 3-c, 4-b

⬍ **Read and mediate on "God's Word for Today" in the margin.**
Spend a moment in prayer as you begin today's lesson.

I grew up in the suburbs, so gardening metaphors would be lost on me if it were not for a couple of summers when my parents decided we needed a garden. Having grown up in the country, they both knew when to till the soil and harvest the vegetables. During those few summers of gardening, I learned an important lesson: it always takes more seeds than I think are necessary.

In gardening the tasks of preparing the soil, tending the sprouts, pulling weeds, watering, and harvesting all take a great amount of effort. In addition, gardening requires a lot of waiting. Sowing seeds, however, doesn't take long. You simply take the seed in your hand and scatter it. It should be that easy for us to spread God's Word.

1. **Read Luke 8:4-8 in the margin and record the four different soils Jesus identified.**

   1. _____ 3. _____
   2. _____ 4. _____

Having identified the types of soil, Jesus went on to teach that the seed is God's Word (see Luke 8:11). We are to be the sower in the story, always ready to spread the gospel. As sowers of God's Word, we need to remember that the seed will fall in different types of soil.

2. **Read Luke 8:11-15 on page 85 and match each soil type with its description.**

   ___ 1. Hard soil on path   a. Seed takes no root.
   ___ 2. Rocky soil   b. Seed takes root and grows.
   ___ 3. Thorny soil   c. Seed is choked by worries of life.
   ___ 4. Good soil   d. Seed is snatched away by the enemy.

We are often tempted to reserve our evangelistic efforts for only those people we consider to be good soil. On the contrary, the sower in Jesus' story still scatters seed in places where it is difficult to take root. Therefore, we should generously sow God's Word in all of our conversations. The Great Commission is an undeniable responsibility shared by all believers. Jesus gives all of us the task of spreading the news of God's gift of new life to everyone—even the difficult people in our lives.

(3) **Rank how easy it is for you to share the gospel in the following circumstances. Let *1* mean *very easy* and *5* mean *very hard*.**

A friend experiencing a family crisis   1 2 3 4 5
A person you just met   1 2 3 4 5
A fellow employee during lunch   1 2 3 4 5
A family member   1 2 3 4 5
A new neighbor   1 2 3 4 5

There are numerous ways we can engage in generous conversations about God's Word.

1. *Begin by simply listening to what others normally talk about.* By gaining insights into their lives, you will prepare your own heart to graciously speak about God's Word to them.

2. *Make God's Word a normal part of your conversations.* Simply knowing that the Bible is not an off-limits subject frees most believers to speak about it more often.

3. *Keep track of the lessons God is teaching you from His Word.* Most likely, He wants you to pass along the same valuable lessons to others who need His guidance.

4. *Invite a response to the gospel.* If you are generous in sowing the seeds of God's Word, be equally generous in working for the harvest from those seeds.

(4) **You probably know people who fall into each of the four types of soil that Jesus described. Turn to page 107 and complete "Seed-Scattering List" by recording the names of people you know who correspond to each of the four soil types.**

Pray for ways to generously sow God's Word into the lives of the people you listed on "Seed-Scattering List."

(5) Identify what God wants you to do first in the lives of those you listed.

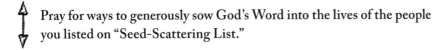

_____

_____

Luke 8:11-15
"This is the meaning of the parable: The seed is the word of God. The seeds along the path are those who have heard. Then the Devil comes and takes away the word from their hearts, so that they may not believe and be saved. And the seeds on the rock are those who, when they hear, welcome the word with joy. Having no root, these believe for a while and depart in a time of testing. As for the seed that fell among thorns, these are the ones who, when they have heard, go on their way and are choked with worries, riches, and pleasures of life, and produce no mature fruit. But the seed in the good ground—these are the ones who, having heard the word with an honest and good heart, hold on to it and by enduring, bear fruit."

Day 3 • Calling the Wayward Home

God's Word for Today

"The gracious hand of his God was on him, because Ezra had determined in his heart to study the law of the LORD, obey it, and teach its statutes and ordinances in Israel."
Ezra 7:9-10

Come, Thou Fount of Every Blessing

"O to grace how great
   a debtor
Daily I'm constrained to be!
Let Thy grace, Lord,
   like a fetter,
Bind my wandering heart
   to Thee:
Prone to wander, Lord,
   I feel it,
Prone to leave the God
   I love;
Here's my heart, Lord,
   take and seal it;
Seal it for Thy courts
   above."[1]

 Read and meditate on "God's Word for Today" in the margin.
Spend a moment in prayer as you begin today's lesson.

From the beginning God has been calling us back. In the garden of Eden God went to look for Adam and Eve. When the Israelites fell prey to sin, God called them to faithfulness through judges, kings, and prophets. Ultimately, Christ came to establish the new covenant between God and humanity through His blood. Now for almost two thousand years God has worked through the church to call us to the same faithfulness.

We need this call because we wander more often than we stay faithful. One of my favorite hymns is "Come, Thou Fount of Every Blessing." Read stanza 3 in the margin. Even when we recognize the great price God has paid for us to know Him personally, we tend to act like wayward rebels.

1) **Check things that often distract believers from faithfulness to God.**
   ○ Temptation to sin   ○ Busy doing other "good" things
   ○ Bad attitudes   ○ Enjoying other parts of our lives
   ○ Lack of focus on spiritual life   ○ Frustration with the church

No matter what the reason, we tend to be wayward. But God is always ready to call us back to Himself, and His Word usually figures prominently in the call for us to return. For example, during the time of Ezra and Nehemiah, the people were busy rebuilding the walls around Jerusalem, recognized by the world as the city of Israel's God. But while they were busy doing good works, their souls were not being fully transformed by God's power. The only thing that could change them was absent from their lives—God's Word.

We can fall into the same trap today. Believers and churches are sometimes so busy doing good things on behalf of God that they neglect His Word. Consequently, they are never transformed by its power.

2) **What are some of the good things you do that might be distracting you from adequate time in God's Word?**

_____

Ezra had served for many years as God's leader in the city of Jerusalem when Nehemiah arrived. Both men wanted to see the people changed far more than they wished to see lumber, nail, stones, and mortar put in place. God's Spirit moved among the people, and they called for God's Word to be read. They stood and listened for six hours (see Nehemiah 8:1-3).

(3) **Read Nehemiah 8:9-10 in the margin and answer the questions.**

How did the people react when the Word was read? _____

How did the leaders respond? _____

When strong conviction of sin settled on the people, the leaders encouraged them to celebrate the strength offered to them by God for future faithfulness rather than mourn the past that had been lost.

The New Testament church faced the challenge of wayward members. In 1 Corinthians Paul taught the church to deal directly with the sin of a man who was acting in a sexually immoral manner (see 1 Corinthians 5:1-13). Paul confronted the church's apathy in dealing with this man and instructed them to remove him from the church fellowship for a transformative purpose—"so that his spirit may be saved in the Day of the Lord" (v. 5). Even severe church discipline has a redemptive aim.

When Paul wrote his second letter to the Corinthians, the life of this wayward child of God had changed. In 2 Corinthians 2:5-11 Paul told the church to accept the man back because his punishment had been sufficient. Paul did not want him to "be overwhelmed by excessive grief" (v. 7).

We must follow this pattern today. God's Word clearly calls us to faithfulness to God, and we should be bold in holding the body of Christ to the biblical standard. God's Word powerfully calls the wayward back to God.

Spend time in prayer for family members and friends who are wandering far from God. Ask Him to bring to mind Bible passages you could share with them to encourage repentance and faithfulness.

(4) **Write this week's Scripture-memory verse in the margin.**

Nehemiah 8:9-10
"Nehemiah the governor, Ezra the priest and scribe, and the Levites who were instructing the people said to all of them, 'This day is holy to the LORD your God. Do not mourn or weep.' For all the people were weeping as they heard the words of the law. Then he said to them, 'Go and eat what is rich, drink what is sweet, and send portions to those who have nothing prepared, since today is holy to our Lord. Do not grieve, because your strength comes from rejoicing in the LORD.' "

1. Robert Robinson, "Come, Thou Fount of Every Blessing," *Baptist Hymnal* (Nashville: LifeWay Worship, 2008), 98.

Day 4 • Caring for Outsiders

 Read and meditate on "God's Word for Today" in the margin.
Spend a moment in prayer as you begin today's lesson.

Obeying God's Word is more than just praying a prayer. It is more than attending church. It is more than holding on to personal morality in the midst of godless societies. It is even more than telling other people what God's Word says. Spreading God's Word includes the way we treat the least in our society. How we care for the powerless gives keen insight into our souls.

1. **What is your normal reaction to a homeless person you encounter?**
   ○ Look away   ○ Desire to help but usually don't   ○ Always help

In "God's Word for Today," Luke 4:18-19, Jesus quoted from Isaiah 61. When Isaiah had delivered God's Word in the eighth century B.C., he had described the joy that would ensue when the Messiah arrived. Now the Messiah was present, and His message was for the outcasts of society. Ancient Rome was no different from our modern society. The poor and powerless are often left to get by. Most people go through life trying to ignore the less fortunate.

2. **Fill in the blanks to describe the ways Jesus fulfilled Isaiah's prophecy.**
   Preach _____ _____ to the poor
   Proclaim _____ to the captives
   Recovery of _____ to the blind
   Set _____ the oppressed
   Proclaim the year of the Lord's _____

Christ came to accomplish these great works. He intentionally showed up on our planet, moved into our neighborhood, and lived among us. Like Him, we need to show up where people are hurting.

3. **Read James 1:27 in the margin. How did James define pure religion?**
   _____
   _____

James described "pure and undefiled religion" as looking after people "in their distress" (v. 27). How can we look after people if we deliberately don't go out looking for them to discover their needs?

④ Check the statement that describes your church.
○ We invite the needy to come to our church building.
○ We go into the community to discover and meet needs.

If we follow Jesus' example, we will not stand around waiting for the needy to show up at our soup kitchens or to meet them by accident. We know they are out there—outside the church and outside our lives. Many are outside God's kingdom.

God cares about widows, orphans, and aliens (see Deuteronomy 10:18), and His Word instructs His people to care for them (see Deuteronomy 24:21). We should be concerned about justice for the powerless in our society (see Micah 6:8).

⑤ Identify people in your community who are powerless. _____
_____

Scripture delivers two mandates for believers today that are based on Jesus' example.
1. Luke 19:10 expresses Jesus' gospel mandate: "The Son of Man has come to seek and to save the lost."
2. Luke 4:18-19 expresses Jesus' cultural mandate to care for outsiders.

Living in God's Word motivates us to show His compassion to people who need help. When we minister to others, we reflect God's image in us, and we gain an opportunity to introduce people to Jesus. As we move out into the fringes of society to care for the elderly who are alone, the immigrant who is afraid, and the imprisoned who need guidance, we must take up both mandates from the life of Christ. My friend Ed Stetzer often says, "We must be a people who carry both Jesus and justice to the world."

Pray about what God wants you to do to begin fulfilling Christ's social mandate. What initial step will you take?
_____
_____

Deuteronomy 10:17-18
"The LORD your God is the God of gods and Lord of lords, the great, mighty, and awesome God, showing no partiality and taking no bribe. He executes justice for the fatherless and the widow, and loves the foreign resident, giving him food and clothing."

Deuteronomy 24:21
"When you gather the grapes of your vineyard, you must not glean what is left. What remains will be for the foreign resident, the fatherless, and the widow."

Micah 6:8
"He has told you men what is good and what it is the LORD requires of you: Only to act justly, to love faithfulness, and to walk humbly with your God."

God's Word for Today

"What you have heard from me in the presence of many witnesses, commit to faithful men who will be able to teach others also." 2 Timothy 2:2

It was a call for Timothy to do what Paul had already done.

Day 5 • Raising Up Leaders

 Read and meditate on "God's Word for Today" in the margin. Spend a moment in prayer as you begin today's lesson.

As a teenager, I surrendered to God's call on my life to become a minister. At that time a young leader in our church began intensely training me to understand how to lead people by God's Word. Matthew remains a dear friend today. The three years of his discipleship and care still influence much of my life.

You see, when Matthew entered the ministry, his pastor spent a lot of time teaching him how to understand a portion of Scripture, apply it, and teach it. Eventually, Matthew instilled those lessons in my life and several other young men's lives. The hope of such an effort is that we will pass along the same lessons to still others. My friendship with Matthew is a modern-day example of the relationship between Paul and Timothy.

When Paul wrote the second letter to Timothy, he was awaiting his own execution by the Roman Empire. From a prison cell he passionately pleaded for Timothy to persevere in trials and to remain faithful to God's Word. It was a call for Timothy to do what Paul had already done.

1. **What leaders helped you understand the Scriptures?**

_____

"God's Word for Today," 2 Timothy 2:2, depicts a progression by which a Christian can pass along God's Word and raise up new leaders.

2. **Refer to 2 Timothy 2:2 in the margin and fill in the blanks to illustrate the progression by which God's Word was to be passed along.**

From Paul to _____ to _____ _____
to _____

First, Timothy and many others heard Paul's teaching. Timothy would entrust the same teachings to others who were faithful. The faithful men whom Timothy taught were, in turn, to teach others also.

(3) **Where do you currently fit in the process? Check one.**
○ Paul ○ Timothy ○ Faithful learners ○ Others

Why do you feel that is where you fit? _____

_____

The church always needs faithful leaders who understand, apply, and teach God's Word to others. We need faithful leaders in our pulpits, Sunday School classes, home Bible studies, student ministries, and children's ministries. Worship leaders and committee members all need to be leaders in handling God's Word. Throughout the church we need people who lead with God's Word as the center of their lives and their ministries.

God's call to be a Christian is a call to be a leader. You do not have to be a pastor to be a leader. You are a leader by virtue of being a member of God's family.

> God's call to be a Christian is a call to be a leader.

(4) **Read 1 Peter 2:9 in the margin and fill in the blanks below to identify our identity as believers.**
We are a chosen _____.
We are a royal _____.
We are a holy _____.
We are a people for His _____.

1 Peter 2:9
"You are a chosen race, a royal priesthood, a holy nation, a people for His possession, so that you may proclaim the praises of the One who called you out of darkness into His marvelous light."

Because your identity is anchored in Christ, your assignment is to "proclaim the praises of the One who called you out of darkness into His marvelous light." You are a leader in God's kingdom who is responsible for living in God's Word and for sharing His Word of truth with others.

(5) Write this week's Scripture-memory verse. _____

_____

_____

Pray and ask God to show you ways He wants you to be a leader in sharing the truth of His Word. Identify anyone He has placed in your life to whom He wants you to pass along the lessons you are learning from His Word.

_____

_____

Session 6 • Spreading the Word

WELCOME AND PRAYER
Welcome participants and pray for God's guidance during the discussion.

OPENING ACTIVITY
1. Invite a participant to recite this week's memory verse.
2. "Follow the Leader" is a game in which children imitate the actions of the leader. What are some silly or crazy ways adults imitate one another (for example, sports fans, coworkers, and fashion trends)?

REVIEW OF DAILY WORK
1. Learning about the Bible often focuses solely on Bible knowledge. How have this week's devotionals challenged that idea?
2. Think about your web of relationships. What friend or family member has contributed the most to your understanding of the Bible? How?
3. This week's memory verse shows a progressive cycle of teaching God's Word. Describe the way the Word is shared. How do you see this pattern working in your church?
4. Read 2 Timothy 2:2. In what respect is every Christian a leader in regard to God's Word? Respond to activity 3 on page 91.

GROUP DISCUSSION

Discover
Throughout this study we have learned that God's Word is His revelation that He has provided for all people. This week we focused on five arenas of life in which you can spread the Word through your relationships. Which of the five ways seems most challenging to you? Why?

Connect
Read Psalm 145:4. Name some of God's "mighty acts" that previous generations of Christians taught you.

Relate
Luke 8:4-15 is the parable of the sower, seed, and soils. How has your own life reflected the four types of soil in response to God's Word? Describe a time when a Scripture penetrated your life and new growth occurred.

Confront

1. What are typical excuses or objections Christians make to avoid talking about the Bible with others? Teaching a Sunday School class or Bible study? Witnessing? Leading a family Bible study?
2. What objection to these spiritual activities do you most often use? How will you overcome these personal objections in order to share God's Word with others?
3. Read Deuteronomy 11:19. Respond to activity 4 on page 83. What are some ways you can teach God's Word to your children?

Change

1. Read Ezra 7:9-10 and Nehemiah 8:9-10. Sometimes religious activity can actually keep us from spiritual growth. How can we guard ourselves from this trap? What role does God's Word play in bringing spiritual transformation rather than religious or social work?
2. What difference does the goal of spiritual transformation make in the way we interact with other people?
3. Read Luke 4:18-19. Identify the two mandates from Jesus' life on page 89. Who are the powerless and needy in your community? How does your church need to respond, according to God's Word?

MISSIONAL APPLICATION

1. Discuss the four ideas for generous conversations on page 85. Share your responses to "Seed-Scattering List" on page 107.
2. Identify ways God's Word calls the wayward home (day 3).
3. Read 1 Peter 2:9. Share the names of people you listed in the prayer activity on page 91. What has God taught you over the past six weeks that you hope to pass along to one of the people you listed?

PREVIEW WHAT'S NEXT

Take time to discuss what other Bible studies or discipleship courses your group would like to study next (for suggestions, see p. 110).

PRAYING TOGETHER

Close the session in prayer for one another.

Outline of the Bible

OLD TESTAMENT

Law
Genesis
Exodus
Leviticus
Numbers
Deuteronomy

History
Joshua
Judges
Ruth
1–2 Samuel
1–2 Kings
1–2 Chronicles
Ezra
Nehemiah
Esther

Poetry
Job
Psalms
Proverbs
Ecclesiastes
Song of Songs

Major Prophets
Isaiah
Jeremiah
Lamentations
Ezekiel
Daniel

Minor Prophets
Hosea
Joel
Amos
Obadiah
Jonah
Micah
Nahum
Habakkuk
Zephaniah
Haggai
Zechariah
Malachi

NEW TESTAMENT

Gospels
Matthew
Mark
Luke
John

History
Acts

Paul's Epistles
Romans
1–2 Corinthians
Galatians
Ephesians
Philippians
Colossians
1–2 Thessalonians
1–2 Timothy
Titus
Philemon

General Epistles
Hebrews
James
1–2 Peter
1–3 John
Jude

Prophecy
Revelation

Spiritual Battle Plan

As Christians, we are in a constant battle with temptation. In week 2 you studied the power of God's Word. You learned that God's Word is our only offensive weapon for the spiritual battle against our enemy and against temptation. Reading, memorizing, studying, or referring to the following Scripture passages will help you fight back when you are tempted.

FEELING OVERWHELMED BY TEMPTATION
Psalm 139
1 Corinthians 10:13
Hebrews 2:18

ANGER
Psalm 37:8
Psalm 145:8
Proverbs 16:32
Matthew 5:22
James 1:19-20

FEAR
Psalm 46:1-2
Romans 8:14-15
2 Timothy 1:7

HOPE
Psalm 42:11
Psalm 71:5
Romans 15:13

HURRY
Psalm 62:1
Psalm 116:7
Psalm 127:2
Mark 6:30-31

JEALOUSY
Exodus 20:17
Proverbs 14:30
1 Corinthians 13:4

LONELINESS
Romans 8:35-39
Hebrews 13:5

PRIDE
James 4:6
1 Peter 1:5-7

SEXUAL TEMPTATION
Proverbs 5:17-23
Matthew 5:27-30
Ephesians 4:19-24
Hebrews 13:4

STRENGTH
Psalm 27:1
2 Corinthians 12:9-10
Ephesians 3:14-19

UNHEALTHY RELATIONSHIPS
Psalm 1:1-2
Proverbs 1:10-19
Proverbs 5:1-14

Guidelines for a Quiet Time

Knowing where to begin is sometimes the most difficult part of a task. Maintaining a daily time with God will require you to make an initial decision about its importance and priority in your daily activities.

1. Make it a priority.

Make your devotional time a priority for life, not just your day. To maintain a consistent personal devotion time with God, you see its importance in the grand scheme of life. After all, spending time with God is a big deal. Entering this time is a daily joy with lifelong benefits and eternal blessings.

2. Choose a place.

A person does not have to be completely cut off from the world to have a devotional time with God. But a quiet spot will help you focus on God's Word, on prayer, and on the Holy Spirit's movement in your life.

3. Choose a time.

I don't know whether one time of the day is superior to another for Bible study and prayer, but there seems to be a natural need to begin our day seeking God's guidance. I recommend that you awaken early enough to begin your day with time for Christ (which also means going to bed earlier too) even if you do your more in-depth Bible study at another time of the day. Block out that time and let your family know what you are doing. You may want to invite them to join you on occasion.

4. Have the right tools at hand.

Obviously, you need to have your Bible. Carefully choose which translation you will use to study and stay with it. Keep a journal or a notebook on hand to write down the ways God is speaking to you through His Word. Recording the lessons He teaches you will aid your spiritual development by reinforcing what you are learning and how you can apply it. Your journal will also become an important record of spiritual markers in your life—times when God reveals Himself to you in meaningful, life-changing ways.

5. Pick a format that works for you right now.

Life is chaotic. One day calls for early meetings and the next for late ones. Keep your dedication to a quiet time as immovable as possible, but be flexible about the format for your quiet time. Different experiences in life and assignments from God will call for different approaches to your time with God.

6. Schedule ample time.

Henry Blackaby frequently uses the phrase "unhurried time with God"[1] to describe his private time with Christ. We should not allow trivial matters to distract us from the great gift of time spent with God. Commit that your time with God will be unhurried.

1. Doy Cave, "God Misses You Too," *Christian Single* [online, cited 11 February 2009]. Available from the Internet: *www.lifeway.com*.

Key Doctrines of the Bible

THE SCRIPTURES

Psalm 119:130; Deuteronomy 31:24-26; Joshua 1:8; Romans 15:4; 2 Timothy 3:15-17; 2 Peter 1:19-21

GOD

Genesis 1:1; Exodus 15:11; Deuteronomy 6:4-5; Psalm 147:5; Matthew 11:27; John 5:17; Romans 1:19-21; 1 Corinthians 12:6; Hebrews 11:6; 12:9; 1 John 4:8, 5:7

GOD THE SON

Isaiah 9:6; Luke 3:22; John 1:1-18; 3:16; 10:30; 20:30-31; Colossians 2:9; 1 John 5:20

GOD THE HOLY SPIRIT

Genesis 1:2; Nehemiah 9:30; Psalm 143:10; Matthew 3:16; Mark 1:10; John 3:34; Acts 4:31; 8:17; Romans 8:10-11,26-27

THE NATURE OF HUMANITY

Genesis 1:26-28; 3:1-24; 5:1-2; Jeremiah 17:9; Romans 3:10-18,23; 8:7; Ephesians 2:3

SALVATION

Matthew 1:21; 4:17; 27:22–28:6; Luke 2:28-32; John 3:3-21,36; 5:24; 17:3; Acts 2:21; 4:12; 15:11; Romans 1:16-18; 3:23-25; 4:3; 10:9-10,13; Galatians 2:20; 3:13; Ephesians 1:7; 2 Timothy 1:12; Titus 2:11-14; Hebrews 5:8-9; 9:24-28; James 2:14-26

THE KINGDOM OF GOD

Isaiah 9:6-7; Jeremiah 23:5-6; Matthew 3:2; 13:1-52; 25:31-46; Luke 8:1; 9:2; 12:31-32; 17:20-21; John 18:36; Romans 8:19; Colossians 1:13; Hebrews 11:10,16; 12:28; Revelation 1:6,9; 5:10; 11:15; 21–22.

THE CHURCH

Matthew 16:15-19; 18:15-20; Acts 2:41-42,47; 5:11-14; 6:3-6; 13:1-3; 14:23,27; 15:1-30; 16:5; 20:28; Romans 1:7; 1 Corinthians 1:2; 3:16; 5:4-5; 7:17; 9:13-14; 12; Ephesians 1:22-23; 2:19-22; 3:8-11,21; 5:22-32; Philippians 1:1; Colossians 1:18; 1 Timothy 2:9-14; 3:1-15; 4:14; Hebrews 11:39-40; 1 Peter 5:1-4; Revelation 2–3; 21:2-3

MISSIONS

Matthew 28:18-20; Acts 1:8; Romans 10:13-15; 2 Timothy 4:5; 1 Peter 2:4-10

BAPTISM AND THE LORD'S SUPPER

Matthew 3:13-17; 26:26-30; 28:19-20; Mark 1:9-11; 14:22-26; Luke 3:21-22; 22:19-20; John 3:23; Acts 2:41-42; 8:35-39; 16:30-33; 20:7; Romans 6:3-5; 1 Corinthians 10:16,21; 11:23-29; Colossians 2:12

For more Scriptures on these and other key doctrines, see the tract *The Baptist Faith and Message* (Nashville: LifeWay Press, 2000).

Lead Subject of Each Bible Book

- Genesis: God creates and relates to us.
- Exodus: God's covenant with the Hebrews
- Leviticus: laws for the Hebrew nation
- Numbers: journey to the promised land
- Deuteronomy: reminding the Hebrews of the law
- Joshua: conquest of the promised land
- Judges: leaders from God
- Ruth: beginning of the messianic family
- 1 Samuel: organization of the kingdom
- 2 Samuel: reign of David
- 1 Kings: division of the kingdom
- 2 Kings: history of the divided kingdom
- 1 Chronicles: reign of David
- 2 Chronicles: history of Southern Kingdom
- Ezra: return from captivity
- Nehemiah: rebuilding Jerusalem
- Esther: escape of Israel from genocide
- Job: problem of suffering
- Psalms: songbook of Israel
- Proverbs: wisdom for living
- Ecclesiastes: finding true meaning in life
- Song of Songs: glorification of wedded love
- Isaiah: messianic prophet
- Jeremiah: last effort to save Jerusalem
- Lamentations: dirge over Jerusalem's loss
- Ezekiel: "They will know that I am the LORD."
- Daniel: difference between kingdoms
- Hosea: God's unrequited love
- Joel: God's judgment of the unfaithful
- Amos: social justice
- Obadiah: destruction of God's enemies
- Jonah: errand of mercy to Nineveh
- Micah: warning against idolatry
- Nahum: destruction of Nineveh

- Habakkuk: "The righteous one will live by his faith" (2:4).
- Zephaniah: approaching day of the Lord
- Haggai: rebuilding the temple
- Zechariah: coming kingdom and King
- Malachi: final message to the disobedient
- Matthew: Jesus the King
- Mark: Jesus the Servant
- Luke: Jesus the Man
- John: Jesus the divine
- Acts: birth of the church
- Romans: Christ's work described
- 1 Corinthians: church in need of love
- 2 Corinthians: church triumphant
- Galatians: triumph of grace over law
- Ephesians: unity of the church
- Philippians: joy in God's mission
- Colossians: deity of Jesus
- 1 Thessalonians: the future return of Christ
- 2 Thessalonians: standing firm in difficult days
- 1 Timothy: caring for the church
- 2 Timothy: Paul's final word
- Titus: defending sound doctrine
- Philemon: conversion of a runaway
- Hebrews: Christ our High Priest
- James: living our faith
- 1 Peter: encouragement to the persecuted
- 2 Peter: prediction of apostasy
- 1 John: fellowship of love
- 2 John: encouragement to remain faithful
- 3 John: commitment to the truth
- Jude: guarding the faith
- Revelation: Christ the victor

You can find more information by reading the book introductions in *The Holman Illustrated Study Bible*.

Scripture-Passage Worksheet

Scripture passage: _____ Date of study: _____

Read the passage slowly.

Respond to God's Word through prayer and meditation.

Review the passage.

Genre type (see pp. 60–61): _____

1. How does this verse or passage reveal God's character? _____
_____
_____

2. How does the passage reveal God's redemptive plan? _____
_____
_____

3. What objections do I raise against the truth found in the passage? _____
_____

4. How did the passage apply to the original hearers? _____
_____

5. How does this truth address my relationship with Christ? _____
_____
_____

Application to make: _____

Verse to memorize: _____

Prayer of commitment: _____
_____

You have permission to duplicate this page for personal use.

Bible-Study Tools

BIBLE TRANSLATIONS

Language usage changes over time. Modern translations of the Bible seek to translate the original Hebrew and Greek texts in ways that clarify the accurate meaning for readers. Because ancient words can be translated differently depending on their contexts, reading the same passage in different translations can add insight or understanding as we study God's Word. Commonly used translations include:

• Holman Christian Standard Bible (HCSB)
• English Standard Version (ESV)
• New International Version (NIV)
• New King James Version (NKJV)
• King James Version (KJV)

Paraphrases like The Message and The Living Bible are different from translations. They reflect the writer's personal interpretations of Scripture by adding to the original text. A paraphrase, like a commentary, can be a meaningful supplement to your study.

AUDIO BIBLE

Many translations are available in audio and download formats for listening convenience.

CONCORDANCE

Many Bibles have a concordance at the back. It lists words and the references where those words are used in the Bible. An exhaustive concordance lists every occurrence of the word. Computer or Internet-based Bible-study tools usually allow you to search for a word and give you the results you would find in a concordance. Using a concordance, you can find out what other Scriptures may have to say about that topic. The most commonly used concordance is *Strong's Exhaustive Concordance of the Bible*. It lists all occurrences of a Bible word and has a numbering system by which you can learn the Hebrew or Greek word being used in a passage.

CENTER-COLUMN OR CHAIN REFERENCES

Some Bibles also list additional references to similar words or topics in a center column, in footnotes, or as a chain of references you can follow by moving from one Scripture reference to another. For instance, if you look at 2 Timothy 2:15, the center-column reference might list Ephesians 1:13, Colossians 1:5, and James 1:18 as additional references for the phrase "word of truth."

An Approved Worker

14 Remind them of these things, charging them before God[a] not to fight about words;[f] this is in no way profitable and leads to the ruin of the hearers. 15 Be diligent to present yourself approved to God, a worker who doesn't need to be ashamed, correctly teaching the word of truth.[g] 16 But

2:12 e Hv 20:4
2:14 f 1Tm 6:4
2:15 g Eph 1:13; Col 1:5; Jms 1:18
2:16 h Jd 18
2:17 i 1Tm 1:20
2:18 j Ac 17:32; 1Co 15:12-17; 2Th 2:1-2 k 1Tm 1:19; 6:21
2:19 l Jos 23:7; Est 9:4; Is 26:13; Rm 15:20; Eph 1:2

STUDY BIBLE

A study Bible includes tools in addition to the Scripture to help you study your Bible. These tools typically include an introduction to each Bible book explaining the context of when and why it was written and by whom.

Notes for verses and topics are included to explain what is meant by the verse and to help you make personal applications. Study Bibles also have a variety of tools that can deeply enrich your Bible learning.

BIBLE DICTIONARY
A Bible dictionary explains the meanings of Bible words, concepts, topics, people, history, and/or geography.

BIBLE HANDBOOK
Handbooks provide background information about the Bible books and text in simple and compact form for introductory study.

WORD-STUDY TOOLS
These books give in-depth analysis of Greek and/or Hebrew words. They describe how words are used in Scripture and in contemporary texts from biblical times.

COMMENTARY
Commentaries come as a single volume or as a whole series of books written to explain the texts in Scripture. Commentary authors are normally scholars who have carefully studied the Scriptures, and they write to help you understand the meaning and application of the Scriptures. Some commentaries are more devotional, while others are more academic.

BIBLE ATLAS
Typically, a Bible atlas includes maps of cities and regions found in the Bible. Sometimes they also include maps of routes taken by certain biblical characters, such as the apostle Paul's missionary journeys. Others may also add photographs of modern Bible locations and archaeological information on Bible sites.

HARMONY OF THE GOSPELS
This tool takes the texts from the Gospels of Matthew, Mark, Luke, and John and provides a chronological comparison of the texts for studying Jesus' life and teachings.

COMPUTER AND ONLINE TOOLS
Many Web sites provide free online Bible-study tools. These include a variety of Bible translations, concordances, dictionaries, commentaries, word-study tools, maps, and devotionals to aid your Bible study. Check out *http://bible.lifeway.com* as a starting place. Computer programs make entire libraries of study material available for more in-depth study.

BIBLE-STUDY WORKBOOKS
Another helpful tool is a Bible-study book or workbook. The author has done much of the study in a variety of resources for you. He or she shares insights in a format that engages you to carefully think and apply the Scriptures to your life through interactive questions and activities. Studies can be topical or can focus on a Bible book. Go to *www.lifeway.com* to discover other discipleship workbooks like this one.

Claude King, *The Call to Follow Christ* (Nashville: LifeWay Press, 2006), 94–95.

Recommended Resources

BIBLE ATLAS
Holman Bible Atlas by Thomas V. Brisco, B&H Publishing Group, 1999.

Holman Book of Biblical Charts, Maps, and Reconstructions by Marsha A. Ellis Smith, B&H Publishing Group, 1993.

BIBLE CONCORDANCE
Holman CSB® Comprehensive Concordance, B&H Publishing Group, 2005.

Strong's Exhaustive Concordance to the Bible, Hendrickson Publishers, 2009.

BIBLE DICTIONARY
Holman Illustrated Bible Dictionary by Chad Brand, Charles W. Draper, and Archie England, B&H Publishing Group, 2003.

Vine's Complete Expository Dictionary of Old and New Testament Words: With Topical Index by W. E. Vine, Thomas Nelson Publishing, 1996.

BIBLE ENCYCLOPEDIA
The Zondervan Pictorial Encyclopedia of the Bible, edited by Merrill C. Tenney, Zondervan Publishing Company, 1975.

The International Standard Bible Encyclopedia, edited by Geoffrey Bromiley, Wm. B. Eerdmans Publishing Company, 1995.

BIBLE HANDBOOK
Holman Bible Handbook by David S. Dockery, B&H Publishing Group, 1992.

Halley's Bible Handbook by Henry Halley, Zondervan Publishing Company, 1961.

BIBLE SURVEY
Old Testament Survey by Paul R. House and Eric Mitchell, B&H Publishing Group, 2007.

The New Testament: Its Background and Message by Thomas D. Lea and David Alan Black, B&H Publishing Group, 2003.

What the Bible Is All About by Henrietta Mears, Gospel Light Publications, 2002.

TOPICAL BIBLE
So That's in the Bible? by John Perry, B&H Publishing Group, 1997.

Holman Concise Bible Concordance, B&H Publishing Group, 1999.

GENERAL REFERENCE
The Treasury of Scripture Knowledge by R. A. Torrey, Hendrickson Publishers, 2002.

WORD STUDIES
Holman Treasury of Key Bible Words by Eugene E. Carpenter and Philip Wesley Comfort, B&H Publishing Group, 2000.

Bible-Reading Plans

Reading the entire Bible might seem like a difficult task, but it is not. Although encountering difficult passages is part of the journey, we should look forward to the lifelong endeavor to understand God's Word.

Below are several plans for reading the Bible as a whole and in parts. Choose one and discover the epic account of God's transformative power in our lives.

THE BIBLE IN A YEAR

Beginning to End
You can read the entire Bible in a year simply by reading three or four chapters each day. The reading can be done from Genesis to Revelation, or you can read two chapters in the Old Testament and one or two chapters in the New Testament each day.

Chronological
Read the events of the Bible as they happened chronologically. This will also require reading three or four chapters each day.

Old and New
Some reading guides use a mix of both Old Testament and New Testament chapters each day. These reading plans add variety to your reading and help you relate the two Testaments relate to each other.

GENRE PLAN
Read a different genre of Scripture each day. For example, read from the Gospels on Monday and from the Law on Tuesday.

SHORTER PLANS
For a more intensive journey through the Bible, you could choose to do it in a shorter amount of time. You can read the entire Bible in three months by covering 13 or 14 chapters each day.

You can choose a slower pace and read a portion of Scripture in smaller amounts of time:
- You can read the Gospels in a month by reading three chapters each day.
- You can read the entire New Testament in 90 days by reading three chapters per day.
- Because there are 150 psalms, you can read the book in a month by reading five each day, with one day dedicated to Psalm 119, the longest chapter in the Bible.

RESOURCES
Numerous resources are available to help you read through the Bible. Here are a few.
- Reading God's Story: A Chronological Daily Bible (HCSB), B&H Publishing, 2001
- Read the Bible for Life Reader's Guide to the Bible: Chronological Reading Plan (HCSB) LifeWay Press, 2001
- *The One-Year Chronological Bible (NIV),* Tyndale House Publishers, 2007

You can also find numerous Bible-reading plans online.

Tips for Memorizing Scripture

Discipleship Helps • Live in the Word

1. Select carefully.

It is easier to memorize information that has immediate application or interest. Choose verses that are related to a topic you are studying or an issue you are facing. As you read your Bible, mark verses you may want to memorize later. Select verses from your pastor's sermon, a small-group Bible study, or a personal study you are working through.

2. Use reference cards.

Write the verse and reference on the front of a card with the reference only on the reverse side. (See the cards at the back of this book.) If you have a computer, type or copy verses into a word-processing program and print them on perforated business cards. Write the date on the card for later reference.

3. Seek understanding.

Context is often the key to understanding a passage, so read the verse in its context (the verses before and after it, such as a paragraph or even a chapter). Utilize tools like Bible dictionaries, concordances, and commentaries to gain a better understanding of the verse you are memorizing.

4. Pray and meditate.

As you read, recite, and commit a verse to memory, make it personal. Repeatedly ask God in prayer how the verse applies to your life and circumstances. During your devotional times, meditate on the truth of the verse and on its insight into the character of God, how He relates to us, and how we can be transformed by His grace.

5. Read the verse aloud.

Practice reading the verse aloud several times each day.

6. Move from small to big.

We often fail at memorization because we try to learn too much at once. Learn to quote the verse one phrase at a time. Memorizing the verse in short phrases will enable you to better learn the meaning of the verse and meditate on it. Continue adding phrases until you can quote the entire verse word for word.

7. Recite aloud.

Invite another person to check your memory as you recite the verse. Explain to them what God is teaching you through the verse.

8. Regularly review the memorized verse.

During rhe first week or two, carry your reference card in your pocket or purse. Pull it out for review several times daily during waiting periods like riding in an elevator, during a coffee or lunch break, or waiting for an appointment. Review the verse at least daily for the first six weeks. Review it weekly for the next six weeks and monthly thereafter.

Prayers of the Bible

OLD TESTAMENT
- Abraham's prayer for Sodom and Gomorrah (Genesis 18:23-33)
- Moses' intercession for the Israelites (Exodus 32:31-32)
- Moses and God's glory (Exodus 33:18)
- Moses' intercession for Miriam (Numbers 12:13)
- Moses' 40-day prayer (Deuteronomy 9:25-29)
- Hannah's prayer for a child (1 Samuel 1:10-12)
- Hannah's prayer of thanksgiving (1 Samuel 2:1-10)
- Solomon's prayer for wisdom (1 Kings 3:6-9)
- Solomon's prayer to dedicate the temple (1 Kings 8:22-53)
- Elijah's prayer for the widow's son (1 Kings 17:20-22)
- Elijah's prayer at Mount Carmel (1 Kings 18:36-39)
- Elisha's prayer (2 Kings 6:15-18)
- Jehoshaphat's prayer for deliverance (2 Chronicles 20:6-9)
- Ezra's confession (Ezra 9:4-15)
- Nehemiah's prayer and fasting (Nehemiah 1:3-11)
- David's prayer for protection (Psalm 3)
- David's prayer for favor (Psalm 4)
- David's prayer for guidance (Psalm 5)
- David's prayer for mercy (Psalm 6)
- David's prayer in persecution (Psalm 7)
- David's prayer for God's help (Psalm 13)
- David's shepherd prayer (Psalm 23)
- David's prayer for trust (Psalm 25)
- David's prayer and fasting (Psalm 35)
- David's prayer for forgiveness (Psalm 51)
- Daniel's prayer (Daniel 9:4-19)
- Jonah's confession (Jonah 2:2-9)

NEW TESTAMENT
- The Model Prayer (Matthew 6:9-13; Luke 11:2-4)
- Jesus' prayer of thanksgiving (Matthew 11:25-26)
- Jesus' prayer for Lazarus (John 11:41-42)
- Jesus' High Priestly prayer (John 17)
- Jesus' prayer in Gethsemane (Matthew 26:39,42)
- Apostles' prayer for divine direction (Acts 1:24,25)
- Apostles and believers' prayer (Acts 4:24-31)
- Stephen's prayer for his murderers (Acts 7:60)
- Paul's prayer for the Ephesians (Ephesians 3:14-21)
- Paul's prayer for the Philippians (Philippians 1:9-11)
- Paul's prayer for the Colossians (Colossians 1:9-17)

Prayer Exercise

There are many ways you can utilize God's Word in your times of prayer. You can use the Word as a model for your prayers, or you can pray the words of Scripture when you don't know what to say to God. The following suggestions will guide you to use Psalm 23 in your prayers today.

¹"The Lord is my shepherd; there is nothing I lack."

Tell the Lord how grateful you are for His presence in your life. Thank Him for the provisions of life, family, work, and the many other good gifts He has given you.

²"He lets me lie down in green pastures; He leads me beside quiet waters."

Talk to the Lord about your need for rest. Listen for the Spirit's movement in your soul about times in life where you should slow down and feed on God's Word.

³"He renews my life; He leads me along the right paths for His name's sake."

What are the decisions you need to make for which you need God's wisdom? Ask the Lord for direction in your life. Also ask Him for wisdom as He uses you to lead others. Thank the Lord that He is always present to lead us, whether we are walking in discouraging or joyful days.

⁴"Even when I go through the darkest valley, I fear no danger, for You are with me; Your rod and Your staff—they comfort me."

Recount to God the times He has strengthened you in desperate times. If you are currently in a dark valley, tell the Lord that you have faith in His power to protect you.

⁵"You prepare a table before me in the presence of my enemies; You anoint my head with oil; my cup overflows."

Respond to God's blessings in your life. When a king anoints someone, it is a sign of his favor. Thank God for welcoming you into His family. Seek His perspective about the enemies you might be facing, such as doubt or temptation.

⁶"Only goodness and faithful love will pursue me all the days of my life, and I will dwell in the house of the Lord as long as I live."

Worship the Lord for pursuing us with His "goodness and faithful love." Praise the Lord at length about all of His wonderful qualities. Tell God how happy you are to be welcomed into His house.

Reread Psalm 23 aloud again, but this time put special emphasis on all of the names and pronouns that refer to God.

End your prayer time by thanking God for His daily presence in your life.

Seed–Scattering List

Week 6 addressed the importance of having generous conversations that sow the truth of God's Word in others' lives. The parable of the four soils (Luke 8:4-8) teaches that we often face different types of people and situations when discussing God's Word. Nevertheless, we are to scatter the "seed" everywhere. List people and places where you need to scatter the seed of God's Word and His gospel.

	People	Places
Hard Soil		
Rocky Soil		
Thorny Soil		
Good Soil		

Leader Guide

If you have not read the introduction beginning on page 7, do so before continuing.

Although you could study this book alone, finding a group of friends to join in a journey through the study will most likely bear more fruit in your life.

GROUP SESSIONS

At each group session participants will follow a suggested process to review the daily lessons and to discuss and apply ideas for living according to God's Word. Session plans are provided at the end of each week's devotionals. Each session includes the following components.

Welcome and Prayer

There is simply no way to overestimate the power of prayer in our lives. Your group should value this time to pray for one another and to submit their lives to God, who speaks through His Word.

Opening Activity

Various methods can be used to get group members to open their lives to one another. Two methods you will use are accountability and humor. For each session you should ask someone ahead of time to recite the memory verse(s) for the week. Try to enlist a different person for each session. This simple act of accountability will encourage deeper commitment from participants.

You can also use humor to encourage interaction. Each week your group will engage in a funny exercise or offer answers to a humorous question to begin the discussion. Learning to laugh together will break down barriers so that members will be willing to share about more serious questions during the session.

Review of Daily Work

In this section participants will review what they learned from the daily devotions. The intention is for the group to discuss the key concepts and find practical applications for the memory verse each week.

Group Discussion

Each week's group discussion is divided into five components:
1. Discover: a key doctrine to discuss
2. Connect: a key Scripture to review
3. Relate: a key narrative passage to observe
4. Confront: a key objection to answer
5. Change: a key challenge to live

These five sections will provide opportunities to dig into the week's lessons and will challenge participants to apply what they learned to their spiritual journeys.

Missional Application

Intellectual knowledge about the Bible is not enough. We must take what we learn from God's Word and apply our lives to God's mission. Each week this section will challenge participants to find ways to obey the Word as missionaries to their world.

Preview of Next Week
Use the introductory page to overview the upcoming week's study.

Closing Prayer
End your group time each week with a prayer of gratitude to God and seeking His grace for one another.

RESPONSIBILITIES OF THE LEADER

Enlisting Participants
Any believer who desires to know more about their faith will benefit from this study. As you form this study group, ask God to open your eyes to see who in your church and circle of friends needs this study. Invite both new and mature believers to participate.

As you enlist participants, give them a book and ask them to study the introduction and week 1 prior to the session.

Your Role as the Leader
You are not required to be a content expert to lead this study. The only requirement is a desire to personally live according to God's Word and to lead others to do the same.

Your role is to facilitate group discussion, share your ideas, and guide members to discuss the information learned. Each week your goal should be to help participants apply God's Word in their lives. Be sensitive to the growth of members who may struggle along the way. If you need assistance, recruit another mature believer to participate as an assistant leader for the group study. Your role is to point people to Christ and reliance on God's Word. You can more effectively do this as you personally live in God's Word.

Time and Schedule
This course is designed for six sessions. The group sessions need to follow the study of the week's daily devotionals. Members need to have books so that they can study the first week's material prior to session 1. If you are not able to distribute books before the first session, plan an introductory session to distribute the books and get to know one another. Allow at least 60 minutes—preferably 90 minutes—for each session. Longer group sessions provide greater freedom for in-depth discussion, personal sharing, and prayer for one another.

Prayer
As the leader, pray for each participant by name each week. During the first week of the study, contact each participant by phone or in person to discuss how you can privately pray for their spiritual growth and personal needs. Prayer is one of the great privileges and responsibilities as we lead God's people. Right now begin praying for those who have already committed to and those who will commit to participating in *Live in the Word*.

The Growing Disciples Series

New and growing believers need a firm foundation on which to build their lives. The Growing Disciples Series provides short-term Bible studies that establish a strong foundation for a life of following Jesus Christ. The series begins with *The Call to Follow Christ*, which introduces six spiritual disciplines. Subsequent studies help believers understand and practice disciplines that strengthen their love relationship with Christ and develop a lifestyle of faithful, fruitful obedience. Watch for the following six-week resources as the series grows:

Growing Disciples: Abide in Christ
Growing Disciples: Live in the Word
Growing Disciples: Pray in Faith
Growing Disciples: Fellowship with Believers
Growing Disciples: Witness to the World
Growing Disciples: Minister to Others

For a free 20-minute Webinar on the series,
go to *www.lifeway.com/growingdisciples*.

The Call to Follow Christ: Six Disciplines for New and Growing Believers by Claude King is a seven-session, foundational resource that introduces the six disciplines in the series. This unique workbook includes a music CD with seven songs sung by Dámaris Carbaugh that will enrich participants' daily 10- to 15-minute interactive devotion/study time. Item 001303666

To order these resources and to check availability,
fax 615.251.5933; phone toll free 800.458.2772;
order online at *www.lifeway.com;* email *orderentry@lifeway.com;*
visit the LifeWay Christian Store serving you; or write to
LifeWay Church Resources Customer Service;
One LifeWay Plaza; Nashville, TN 37234-0113.